HELD AND FREE

HELD AND FREE

COMING OUT OF YOUR STORY

MEAGAN O'NAN

NEW DEGREE PRESS
COPYRIGHT © 2023 MEAGAN O'NAN
All rights reserved.

Cover art: Derek Kaplan   www.derekkaplan.com

HELD AND FREE
Coming Out of Your Story

ISBN   979-8-88926-622-8   Paperback
        979-8-88926-801-7   Hardcover
        979-8-88926-623-5   Ebook

For Clare. For Merit.
To the family I never imagined
I would have.

CONTENTS

	AUTHOR'S NOTE	11
PART I	**OWN**	**17**
	CHAPTER 1	19
	CHAPTER 2	29
	CHAPTER 3	35
	CHAPTER 4	43
	CHAPTER 5	53
	CHAPTER 6	63
	CHAPTER 7	73
	CHAPTER 8	81
	CHAPTER 9	91
PART II	**SHARE**	**101**
	CHAPTER 10	103
	CHAPTER 11	113
	CHAPTER 12	123
	CHAPTER 13	129
	CHAPTER 14	135
	CHAPTER 15	143
	CHAPTER 16	153

PART III	**CONNECT**	**161**
	CHAPTER 17	163
	CHAPTER 18	171
	CHAPTER 19	181
	CHAPTER 20	189
	CHAPTER 21	195
	EPILOGUE	203
	ACKNOWLEDGMENTS	207
	APPENDIX	211

Held and Free:

The Universe holds my hopes and dreams

gracefully in its hands

while leaving it

to me to trust and receive.

This is my story,

my attempt to understand

why things have happened the way they have

and why I believe I am held and free.

AUTHOR'S NOTE

In the summer of 2004, my life changed. Word got out that I was gay, and a feeding frenzy ensued. People began pressuring me, needing to understand why I had suddenly "decided" I was gay. Everyone was accustomed to perfection from me, but the heaviness was making my knees buckle. All I wanted was to stand tall in my truth. Even though I knew it was a bad idea, I tried to answer everyone's questions. *Are you really gay? How long have you known? Don't you think you are going to go to hell?*

I had to prove to them my life was worthy of acceptance. I had to walk the line so they wouldn't have an excuse to demonize me.

The damning responses to my revelation made me realize my defenses were falling on deaf ears. *I wasn't Christian enough. I had forgotten who God was. I was disgusting, a sinner, a hypocrite.*

I was going to hell, alone and defeated.

At twenty-two years old, I had a vision for how my life would look, and this wasn't it. I was supposed to be with a man and have a family. I was supposed to get married. I wanted to have a daughter and name her Merit. I wanted to be a successful speaker and author. I wanted to love who I was.

How could I do all of that if I were gay, especially in a place that isn't exactly known for its acceptance of anything outside of heteronormativity?

I didn't know any successful gay people at the time—none that were out, anyway. The ones I did know were angry and stuck in the victimhood they felt they deserved. I didn't know any gay people who thought life was on their side. That wasn't who I wanted to be, but I did not yet know the level of shame and unworthiness that was being shoved into the crevices of my heart, the kind of unworthiness that taints your decision-making, camouflaging misfits as missing pieces.

I was an outsider to the life I had known and an outsider to the life I did not yet know.

I spent many years searching for worthiness within myself. I was angry, hurt, insecure, and uncertain about what my life would look like as a gay woman in a straight world below the Mason-Dixon line.

Feeling different than those around you isn't particular to those who are LGBTQ+, and neither are loneliness, isolation, and powerlessness. Health insurer Cigna's 2018 US Loneliness Index found "46 percent of Americans report feeling lonely sometimes or always, and 47 percent report feeling left out sometimes or always. A little less, 43 percent, report feeling isolated from others, and the same number report feeling they lack companionship and that their relationships lack meaning." A 2021 study from Harvard states, "Young adults suffer high rates of both loneliness and anxiety and depression. According to a recent CDC survey, 63 percent of this age group are suffering significant symptoms of anxiety or depression."

Anyone who ever feels like an outsider and wants to create more acceptance and unity in the world understands this dilemma: You are fueled by a fire within to make a difference, but changing others is impossible work. So you get burned out. You feel hopeless. You feel powerless. At some point, you realize the outward work has to become inward if you are going to retain any joy at all.

The question then becomes, "How do you make an impact and stand up for a cause without feeling like you need to change who other people are?"

My answer was to share my story.

I've told my coming out story and shared my personal struggles over and over throughout the years on my blog, on the news, on Mississippi Public Radio, on stages and in classrooms at Mississippi State, in one-on-one conversations behind closed doors, in the grocery store, and even on Facebook Messenger. It has never been my intention to change people's minds with regard to their beliefs about whether being gay is right or wrong. I know what it feels like for people to try to change who you are.

I wanted to find a way to love myself, and sharing my story fulfilled my need to unburden my heart and gave me an opportunity to connect with others in powerful ways. I wanted to understand, and I wanted to be understood. In order to get both, I had to be vulnerable and willing to receive love. We need authentic connection in order to thrive. But someone has to take the first step.

Retrospectively, I see clearly that sharing my stories in a vulnerable way has not only given me a feeling of wholeness in my life now but it has also shown me the value of vulnerable storytelling in building bridges and creating connections. Ultimately, I have found connection and understanding provide a foundation for change to prevail, as they open doors to a kind of cooperation that doesn't involve changing other people's beliefs. By seeking self-acceptance, by being open and vulnerable, I have received acceptance in a community I never thought would embrace me again.

It hasn't been an easy path; healing never is. It has been forged through vulnerability, hard conversations, fountains of tears, a willingness to be seen, and an active, conscious effort to meet people where they are, even when part of me hesitates to show such grace.

Of all the ways I could effect change, I've settled on vulnerable storytelling as my tool of choice. Through owning my story, I've learned how to accept myself and meaningfully connect with others. Those connections have the potential to nurture transformation for everyone involved. Telling my story sometimes feels like the most dangerous type of exposure, but the means justify the desired end. I want to be the representation I needed when I came out, not just for those who are like me but for those who want to understand people who are not like them.

As I walk forward in my day-to-day life, my sense of wholeness becomes more and more complete. But pulling yourself together is like assembling a group of friends to help you move into a top-floor apartment with no elevator. It's hard.

Despite its difficulties, vulnerable storytelling continues to give back. Sharing what I go through allows me to move on, let people in, and create meaning and purpose through every experience.

The Universe holds all of my hopes and dreams gracefully in its hands, all while leaving it to me to trust and receive all it has to offer. Sharing my story over the years in Mississippi has been the driving factor behind this ever-evolving journey toward feeling whole and less alone. There has been heartbreak and loss, fear and courage, disappointment and tough lessons, all leading to me telling my story—this story. This is my attempt to understand why things have happened the way they have and why I believe I am held and free.

PART I

OWN

I had to own what I had been through by accepting my stories as they were.

CHAPTER 1

I sank into the cushions and looked out the window at the still, quiet lake. I wanted what the lake had. When I realized the only way to get that would be to let go of the expectations I had for myself and the people I loved, I sobbed. There were no words, just tears.

Eventually, I got the courage to speak. When I was little and something was bothering me, I would go silent when my mom asked what was wrong. I would just look at her, stunned, eyes glazed over. If I voiced my emotions aloud, they'd become real, and that was scary. But this time, I had to be real. I didn't feel like I had a choice. Contentment was at risk.

In between sobs, I looked down at the floor and pushed the words past the lump in my throat. "I am not who you think I am. I am different than (from) most girls."

My mom gripped my hand. Her eyebrows almost touched when she asked, "What do you mean?"

I mumbled something about not liking boys.

In that instant, my mom's wrinkled forehead stretched to smooth, and as her eyes grew bigger, I could sense her shock. She let go of my hand as my white knuckles were turned pink. "You mean you are gay?"

The look on my mom's face was everything I had wanted to avoid. She looked away from my eyes and down at the ground, then froze for a moment. When she came to, she put her hands on her face and shook her head. Her silence left my mind reeling. What was she thinking? Was she disappointed? She was disappointed. Judging from our complex emotional bond, I figured she was asking herself, "How in the hell are we going to get through this? Who are you, and what have you done with my daughter?"

My mom held me in her arms as I cried, and she repeated that we were going to figure it all out. She didn't reject me. She didn't push me out into the world on my own. Instead, she called my dad so we could sit in the mess together. When he answered the phone, she told him that I told her I was gay. Dad raced home, came in, and sat on the couch across from me. His tough, six-foot-two exterior melted into the cushions as confusion wrinkled his forehead. I could feel my heart about to beat out of my chest at the thought of disappointing him.

He rubbed his eyes as if he were exhausted and then looked at me directly. "Aren't you worried you are going to go to hell?" His Catholic upbringing was speaking for him. I froze for a moment. I had always had a fiery relationship with my dad.

We ached to love one another deeply, but our walls of defense often spoke before we let any love in. "I don't believe in hell." Finally, an honest phrase about what I believed had popped out of my mouth. My dad leaned back, uncrossed his legs, and sighed. My parents seemed unsure of what I meant and shaken by my statement because there was nothing more said about hell. My dad didn't say much more.

I couldn't sense what he was experiencing as he sat silently. I defaulted to the only feeling that my insecurities knew: not feeling good enough. Guilt and shame welled up in my chest. I felt responsible for the sadness and grief and the change my family was about to have to go through if we were going to make it in an opinionated, unaccepting society. How would people treat me? How would they treat my family? Would I be able to be honest about myself now? Would they be able to be honest about me?

I'd been living with this for a while, so my shock had dulled over time, but I thought of how I had felt after I kissed a girl for the first time. I had felt liberated and confined simultaneously. I was free, but no one could know. I am sure my parents felt something similar. They suddenly were aware of a part of me they hadn't seen, but it had to be kept a secret, at least from everyone outside of my immediate family. My mom needed her family together, so she called my brothers and asked them to come home. I had actually told my younger brother, Aaron, months before. I'd known his response would be loving, and it was. He was surprised when I told him, but he hugged me tight, and he made me feel safe. I know it was hard for him to make the adjustment, but he did it with grace and love.

My older brother, Seth, and I were not exceptionally close in childhood—not like Aaron and I were. A lot of the time, it felt like we lived in two different worlds. I constantly sought his acceptance and stood firmly in my own insecurities, doubting that he loved or even liked me. I wasn't sure how Seth would react to my news. He had a tough exterior and was usually hard to read. As adults and friends now, I know he's strong and endearing, and I love him so much for it. But at the time, I was terrified of his response. His thoughts about me meant just as much as my parents' did.

Seth didn't say a whole lot when he came home to be with the family. He was living and working in Starkville, so it didn't take him long to get to the house. After a short hug, he stepped back, giving himself the room to look right into my eyes. I was completely unsure of what he was going to say. With a squeeze of my shoulders, he said the words I would never be able to unhear. "You should consider moving away from Mississippi. It'll be easier for you."

More tears were right behind my eyes, but I couldn't muster the courage to be vulnerable in front of him. Leave my home? It was clear the support I needed wasn't going to come from my family or my hometown, at least not yet. I wanted someone to tell me it was going to be okay, that we would get through this together and they had my back, but they weren't ready to give me that yet. Was there enough strength inside of me to get through this on my own? If I left Mississippi, who would I become?

I knew it was my big brother talking, wanting me to be safe, but there was a part of me that felt like it would have been easier for everyone if I just disappeared. No one would have to face anything, none of the hard stuff. Even I wouldn't have to face a lot of it—at least, not right away.

When I left my parents' house that day, I felt an emptiness that was quickly filling up with humiliation. Hungover from vulnerability, I came to grips with the fact that I was responsible for this major shift in everyone's life—responsible for forcing each of my family members to face something really hard. It was a burden, and in the coming years, the burden would make me angry. While my mom made it clear with her words that she loved me and that we were all going to figure this out together, everything about my announcement still felt heavy and oppressive.

On the drive back to my house, I began thinking about how my life would look going forward. Thoughts of my upbringing and what I knew about my parents kept etching their way into my muddled perspective.

My parents grew up in Kentucky and met in high school. At the time, my mom was fifteen and my dad was sixteen. They were introduced through my dad's younger sister and fell in love. They are in love to this day, over fifty years later, and my mom has all the letters my dad wrote to her in high school.

My mom grew up in northwestern Kentucky in the 1950s and '60s with a close-knit extended family, spending weekends and holidays with her cousins and grandparents. Her home life with her parents and brothers was what you would expect in that day and age in that part of the country. Mom's dad was in charge of all decisions, including what to wear and eat, and mom's mom, also true to the times, kept her feelings to herself. None of that seemed out of the ordinary to my mom. Life was about as normal as anyone else's, until one day, it suddenly wasn't. A woman my mom's age showed up uninvited on their doorstep with a baby.

It was my grandfather's.

In an instant, my mom's family life changed forever. My grandfather went back and forth between my grandmother and the other woman, my grandmother never realizing she had the power to move on and create a new life for herself. It was a tumultuous ride for my mom and her brothers. My grandmother's mindset fell victim to the circumstances, so even when I was a child, I could feel her bitterness. The beliefs that she had no control, that life was against her, and that she could never have what she wanted fueled her unhappiness.

Those circumstances transformed my mom in a different way. Since she'd watched her family break apart, she's always strained her knuckles to keep her own family together, gripping what is so there would be a what if. She's never been so naive to think nothing would ever change, but she never liked it when it did. Even when her parents weathered the storm of my grandfather's infidelity, Mom took it upon herself to pick up the pieces for everyone. As the stability of her parental figures slipped away, so did their emotional availability and reliability.

Mom was nineteen when she and Dad married. He became her safe place. Dad was the one person she felt like she could count on no matter what. Her ultimate dream, along with having a solid and strong marriage, was to be the mom and grandmother of kids who stuck together. Until I came out, we were all on track to help her fulfill that dream. The last thing I ever wanted to do was break up my mother's image of how she wanted her family to be. If I was gay, how would I give her grandchildren?

My dad grew up with seven other siblings in a three-room house. They lived on a farm, and all the children vied for their parents' attention and love. My dad's mom had a new baby every other year, so there was never enough time for her to savor any special bond between herself and each child. My dad's dad was gone a lot working, often gambling away the little money the family had, so the parenting was left up to my grandmother and the older siblings. My dad's family put men at the top of the hierarchy. The men of the house would shake their glass at the dinner table when they wanted one of the women to get up and fill it for them.

My dad has worked for every penny he has ever had. He worked at a local grocery store stocking shelves and bagging groceries while going to college full time so he and my mom could afford to have a life of their own. It was important to him to be a reliable provider for my mom and their new life, a pressure he has continued to put on himself to this day. There's a quiet insecurity about him. I suspect it's because he's always had high expectations of himself and wasn't assured as a child that he could be anything he wanted.

Even so, my dad had a natural drive to make something of himself, and those expectations landed on me. Maybe it was because I was the only girl in the family, but it was always clear he expected me to be something or someone special. I didn't want to disappoint.

Because of their upbringings, my parents' need grew to create something new for their lives. I don't think they ever intended to move away from everything they knew, but an opportunity presented itself years into their marriage with three children in tow.

When I was around eight years old, my parents moved us from Henderson, Kentucky, to Starkville, Mississippi. The transition was traumatic for me. We went from a world I knew backward and forward to one I didn't understand. My parents wanted a better life for us all, one where my dad wouldn't have to work such long hours. My mom was a stay-at-home mom, and that continued once we moved to Mississippi.

I cried every morning until the teacher would call my mom to come get me. My mom would hold me and rock me until I calmed down enough to get through the rest of the day. I was in the third grade and felt completely displaced and alone. The crying went on for two weeks before I began to get comfortable in my new surroundings.

That scared little girl who moved to Mississippi with my family emerged again as thoughts of my parents and my upbringing disappeared and a new fear began to swim in my belly.

I was aware of how hard my parents had worked to provide us with something different. I also noticed the way they simultaneously tried to preserve parts of their upbringing as they opened themselves up to new ways of thinking. The love, tenderness, and compassion I felt from them was laced with a sense of responsibility to become who they had imagined I would be.

I tried to avoid screwing up at all costs no matter what I was doing. Working hard was never my issue. Commitment was never my issue. A fear of failure—a fear of not living up to who my parents wanted me to be—was my greatest self-imposed expectation. I was not about to make a grade below my capabilities, fail in a sport, or do anything else that might diminish the standing I imagined I held in their perception of me.

At the end of my college athletic career, after working all those years to make them proud, I knew I had disappointed my parents in the most profound way possible. I'd had gay coaches and teammates, and it was clear neither of my parents fully accepted them. They embraced my gay teammates, but they certainly wouldn't have chosen "that life" for their one and only daughter. I didn't approve of my teammates either—or maybe I projected that onto my coaches and teammates to protect myself from the fact that was who I was as well. Either way, this news was just as much of a shock to my family as it had been to my friends and teammates, if not more.

The long drive back to my house finally ended, but my mind continued to race. My heart was open and broken. I was unsure about my future—about everything—and burst into tears for what seemed like the millionth time that day. The exhaustion set in, and as I laid down to go to sleep, my tears fell as I closed my eyes. I've tried not to let my coming out process define me, but in a lot of ways, it has. Wavering between beauty and sadness has been my go-to. Climbing out of my own numbness has defined my journey, and the belief that life was on my side and hope was somewhere close has been the rope around my waist.

You can know something and not yet believe it. I went searching for wholeness, but I didn't know that was what I was looking for. Regardless of the choices that kept me running away from myself, wholeness was more determined to find me than despair. Taking an honest look at my traumas and tragedies has been my way out of that despair and opened me up to the possibility that I could, one day, be whole.

CHAPTER 2

As the rumor mill spread word of my coming out, my phone's buzzing in my pocket became more frequent. I took my phone out, knowing more disappointment and nosiness were incoming. It was Darius, one of the leaders of the Fellowship of Christian Athletes, my spiritual family within the athletic community. I hesitated to answer, but I was so sick of being talked down to by others all day that I took the call to prove my life was worthy of acceptance.

"I heard you're gay? Are you datin' a girl? You can't do that, it's a sin. You wanna go to hell?" Darius's loud, sharp voice was demanding answers, which was on par for how he communicated with everyone. Since he was as big as he was assertive, people often relented to what he had to say.

His words were piercing. I pulled the phone from my ear to gather myself. I wanted to hang up, but I talked myself into standing up instead.

"You don't understand. I don't have to explain anything to you."

He insisted, "Meet me at the chapel in ten."

Frustrated and desperate for someone to hear me, I gave in to the pressure and agreed to meet.

It was Mississippi hot that day—an all-encompassing humidity that created trails of sweat down my back behind my sports bra. Shame and sadness walked with me across Mississippi State's pristinely manicured campus as phone call after phone call kept coming in. I stopped answering. My insides wouldn't stop churning as I kept looking over my shoulder to see who was going to be coming at me next.

My heart dropped to my stomach as I arrived at the Chapel of Memories. The chapel had always been a sacred place for me, a place where I could sit and listen for answers. Growing up in the Catholic Church had taught me about the importance of ritual and reverence, but this didn't feel like reverence. I arrived at the chapel first and sat down at one of the wooden pews on the right in the back.

A prayer was inside of me somewhere, but I couldn't find it for the knots in my gut. I stared at the rainbow of colors on the stained-glass windows and wiped sweat from my forehead as I waited for my mentor to arrive. I closed my eyes briefly, but I couldn't breathe. My attempted prayers were empty and forced. I was quiet, but any whisper of hope was silent. The walls around me, which once felt safe, suddenly felt like they were closing in on me while my heart was closing off to the world.

The doors opened behind me, and there they were: Darius, his wife, and their newborn baby. I really loved them, but I wasn't sure if the feelings were still mutual. Where they used to see a friend, they now saw a project. As they inched closer, I sunk into the pew like a child who had greatly disappointed their parents. I felt myself shrinking into invisibility.

They sat down and immediately started quoting Bible verses to me.

"For the wages of sin is death, but the gift of God is eternal life in Christ Jesus our Lord" (Romans 6:23).

I knew the rhythm of conversation and lingo of converting people and keeping them within the reigns of righteousness. I'd been on the giving end before. So this quote didn't make me question being gay. It just made me sad. I was no longer a soul or even a face—just a label.

I sat quietly, and as tears started to swell in my eyes, I looked down quickly to avoid showing them my vulnerability. When I first arrived at the chapel, I had every intention of proving to them there was nothing wrong with me and that I loved my girlfriend. How could there be anything wrong with love between two people?

They lectured on, "The Bible says that if you continue to participate in a homosexual lifestyle, you will burn in hell."

They were trying to scare me, but hell was already all around me. It had chased me all day in every conversation like this one. These bringers of "truth" seemed urgently concerned for the life I would live after I died rather than my well-being in the moment. I just needed a hug. I continued to sit there silently. I tuned out what I could, but the parts I heard followed me around for days to come. At some point, I went numb. All I could hear was the rumbling of voices. Something in me knew to check out to keep myself from completely breaking down.

I glanced up to the front of the church and saw Jesus hanging on the cross. Right then, I felt closest to him. He knew what it was like to be cast aside, to not be seen for who he was. For a moment, we shared that pain. I had been told he faced it all so bravely. But what if he were just like me, melting into the moment because there was nowhere else to run and hide?

I understood then what forgiveness was going to mean for me. I would have to show grace to people who claimed to love me but turned their backs on me. I would have to absolve myself of not having the courage to be authentic sometimes. I would need the fullness of my strength to battle the struggles that were coming down the pike. Forgiveness seemed like something tangible that I might be able to reach out and touch, yet our embrace would be years in the making. It was going to be an uphill battle, and I wasn't sure if that was a mountain with a summit.

All I could hear was my heart breaking as my voice remained stuck in my throat and tears swelled behind my eyes. The worst was happening. Who I was beyond my label of being gay didn't matter anymore. It didn't matter I was a standout two-sport athlete or an athlete who had received every high moral and character award from every team I had ever been on or an Academic All-American or a community service awardee or the once-looked-up-to person who brought athletes together to talk about life and our challenges. None of those things counted anymore.

What was I even doing sitting here listening to this lecture? Why did I show up? Why didn't I just leave?

Because as much as I didn't want to, I cared about what other people thought about me.

Suddenly, a warm hand touched my arm. I caught the eyes of both of my mentors as the man asked me, "Are you still in a relationship with a woman?"

With my head down and a sick feeling in my stomach, I lied. "No."

"Okay," they said. "Let's pray, and you can be on your way."

They said a prayer that I don't remember the words to—something about me being saved from damnation.

As we got up and walked outside, they hugged me. I halfway reached my arms around each of them. Their looks of concern had turned to satisfaction as their prayers had seemed to work. They were under the impression their leadership had led me to salvation, yet the only salvation I really needed was from the people telling me I needed to be saved. Well, that, and I was also on the way to needing saving from myself—though certainly not in the way they thought.

Lying was becoming a way to survive.

A part of me died that day. I lost my hope in others and a belief in myself. Lying about not having a girlfriend wounded me.

I had already started dating shame, but now we were inching closer toward a lifelong commitment. As much as I had every right to feel like the people slandering and questioning me were responsible for the guilt I felt, the weight on my shoulders made me feel responsible for it all.

How was I supposed to deal with this lack of self-worth? I was alone. There wasn't anyone there to say, "This is how you walk through this." My toolkit was empty.

I was going to have to face the tirades from other people who were becoming my internal voice. *You are wrong. You are disgusting. You are not enough. You are a failure. You are a liar. You are less-than.*

I went home after this encounter, shut myself in my room, and began writing to filter out everything that had come at me once the word had gotten out. Putting pen to paper took me back to my childhood when my story with God began.

CHAPTER 3

When I was a kid, the thought of going to church on Sunday mornings made me woozy.

It wasn't the story of Jesus that turned my stomach, but the thought of spending part of my weekend in a somber building where the overarching theme of each homily was our unworthiness—unless, of course, it was Palm Sunday, Easter, or Christmas. Those days were fine, but the other forty nine services of the year felt dark and long. Our priest was a saint, and I loved him so much, but the redundancy of mass made it feel meaningless.

The air of condemnation wasn't my only hang-up. Additionally, I was confused by the fact that women couldn't have a place in church leadership. If they could have, then I might have become a priest so that I could have changed the way mass worked. I would have tried to make the cadence of the service more lively and welcoming. I would have changed the underlying vibe of fear to one of hope. And during the part of the prayer that stated, "I am not worthy of receiving you," I probably would have encouraged my parish to do what I did: stay silent.

Growing up, church felt like a funeral, probably because my family sat in front of the seven-foot tall, crucified Jesus dangling from the rafters. I always wondered what it was like to be crucified for being different. Somehow, in that little body of mine, I could relate. I'm not sure how or why, but I understood his choice to remain true to himself despite the outcome. He accepted his destiny. His sacrifice made sense.

When I would kneel to pray, the statue would come to life in my mind, and while acceptance covered me in those brief moments, there was a condemning voice inside telling me I was supposed to pray harder. It was the voice of what I had been taught about how to pray. *Kneel down, squeeze your eyes shut, and don't open your eyes so everyone will think you are praying hard.* I wanted everyone to know I was praying the right way. I was sure they were all watching.

As much as I loved our church community growing up, I was unsettled by the messages I was receiving. I wasn't aware of it at the time, but I think that is why the headaches started showing up. My body couldn't reconcile that I was not worthy of God's love. The whole idea of my sins having to be forgiven through a priest did not make sense either. Couldn't I just talk to God on my own? We were close.

My mom didn't let me off the hook with my headaches, but I could tell she was trying to understand why I wanted to get out of going to the service. When I was around eight years old, I began pondering a question that popped in my head.

Feeling as though I was teetering at the edge of a cliff, I thought, *It has to end at some point.*

The feeling was one of vastness, so vast that I couldn't contain the fear that sent me running to my mom's room. I shook her awake, and when she turned over, I stuffed my head into her stomach and started crying.

"What's wrong? Did you have a bad dream?"

I shook my head no, but I didn't know what to say.

She got out of bed and walked me to her bathroom so she could turn a light on without waking up my dad. She sat on the toilet and motioned for me to come over. We were eye-to-eye, and she asked me again, "What's wrong?"

I don't remember really talking about things before this point, and it was hard for me to speak or put into words what I was feeling, so I just asked her the question that popped into my head while I was in my bed.

"What happens to time after we die? It has to end at some point, right? Then what happens?"

She was clearly rattled. "I don't know," she answered.

I felt like the only answer to my question was that there was a black void we all fall into at some point. I kept crying. My mom held me until the feelings passed, then I climbed into bed and let her hold me through the night.

The feeling of being held by God is one I understand because of my mom. I misconstrued that feeling of safety for fear because of what I had learned and seen at church: to be afraid of God's judgment instead of engulfed by his love. I still went to bed often with this overwhelming feeling of knowing that the unknown was vast and possibly scary, but my mom's responses counteracted my unsettledness. She never had any answers for my questions or lack thereof, but she did always envelop me during my bouts of fear.

I imagine it was at that moment I began to understand God's love is a lot like my mother's love—constant and eternal and unconditional.

Time went on, and the headaches stopped. I realized I wasn't going to get out of church, so I might as well accept it. I never loved it, but I loved the people in it, and that made going to mass tolerable. Any time I questioned why a prayer was said a certain way, the answer from my mom or dad was usually, "That's just the way it is."

The messages that shaped my world from my early years in church were: we must suffer, we are not worthy of God's love because we are sinners, we must constantly ask for forgiveness, and men are more worthy of God's love than women. And fear. Lots of fear.

Despite that, church wasn't just about fear for me. I also took something from all those Sundays that is still important to me: a sense of community.

My teen years were marked by heavy involvement in our church. I was a big part of our all-girls Bible study, which became more of a social gathering centered around discussions about the mysteries of life. We transformed into a support group of sorts, especially when we all went through the same tragedies.

From 1997 to 1999, our high school lost three different students in three different car accidents. Although I had been to funerals and lost family members before, these experiences were different. They shifted my perception of life. To see lifeless teenagers in their coffins shattered my youth that had once felt secure. I knew Hannah and Chris, so their deaths impacted my view of the fragility of life, but Kayln was a close friend. Her death left me in disbelief.

I drove to her family's house a few blocks away from where everyone gathered—friends, parents, teammates. The swift hand of death gripped each of our realities and tossed us into our own new courses of loss and disarray.

The night I found out about Kayln, I didn't sleep. Restless darkness pestered me until I listened to the voice within calling me to speak at her funeral. I poured my heart out in front of that crowded church. I wanted to comfort the family in some way. I wanted to comfort the community. I wanted to find a way for us to come together in the midst of tragedy and sadness. I wanted her memory to live on through my words. I don't remember what I said, but I remember wanting to be strong.

After speaking, I walked down from the podium past her coffin. Sorrow took over. I sat in a pew after the service and broke down.

My dad came up behind me and held me. "I know there isn't anything I can say that will make you feel better. All I can say is this too shall pass."

Inside, I knew he was right. Time would go on. Eventually, the hurt would begin to diminish.

A light went out for me the year Kayln died. I had just graduated high school and was looking forward to my freshman year on a full basketball scholarship. Kayln died on July 5, and I was set to go to college in August. Between the time she died and I left for school, I was asked to play in the Mississippi North/South All-Star Game because I had been awarded all-state honors.

I didn't have any confidence. I was sad. I was questioning how God could take people in such tragic ways at such young ages and whether life would be full of suffering from then on. Kayln wasn't my sister, Chris wasn't my son or brother, Hannah wasn't my best friend, so I remember feeling like my sadness didn't matter, that it wasn't legitimate because I wasn't the one experiencing the greatest loss. Not knowing how to express or deal with my grief crushed my spirit, but somehow, life was supposed to go on.

I barely played in the all-star game. For most everyone else, it was just another day, but I was trying to breathe in a world that felt like it was closing in on me. In the few minutes I was on the court, I missed every shot I took, I kept turning the ball over, and my legs were heavy with sadness. I looked in the stands to see my parents and my future head coach only to see uncertainty and concern on their faces. All I wanted was to run off the court and cry.

Those feelings followed me onto my college campus. It was too much change too fast, and if my parents and I had known any better, I'd have been in counseling instead of freshman orientation.

So much of my identity leading up to college was wrapped up in being a great athlete. I found my confidence through sports. As I entered college depressed, my performance suffered. I felt like I was disappointing everyone. I began questioning my worth. If I couldn't be the athlete I wanted to be, who was I? I took grief with me my freshman year, and the only place I knew to start finding answers to the questions I was battling was my evolving faith.

I joined the Fellowship of Christian Athletes and began to observe what faith looked like through other people's eyes. I couldn't seem to connect to God like others did when they would close their eyes, raise their hands, and sing during praise and worship time. I didn't feel worthy of God's love like they did. I wasn't raised in a church that taught me I was lovable or worthy as I was.

My questions anchored me to the bottom of a dark sea. Time was swallowing me up as I became hyperaware that in any moment, I could die or someone else I loved could die. Fear took on a new meaning for me. It wasn't just about the fear of death. It was now about the fear of not living fully. I found myself in a cycle of fear, sadness, and judgment of that sadness.

I was trying to make sense of the fragility of life by looking for answers through my faith. The vastness of eternity feels an awful lot like depression: confusing, profound, and endless. My freshman year of college didn't turn out the way I had envisioned it, but I survived. For the first time, I consciously felt unworthy. From there, life took a turn that I wasn't expecting.

CHAPTER 4

Being a good believer means mission trips, so I connected with organizations that combined my faith with sports—the perfect fit.

During my first basketball tour in the Czech Republic and Poland with Athletes in Action, I was asked if I had been saved. I gulped down the panic in my throat and said yes because what if I had said no? What would have happened? Would there have been a ceremony? Would they have all circled around and prayed over me? Would I have been deemed unworthy or less than until my rite of passage was complete?

I decided to play along and dive in headfirst because, had I not, I was sure they would have sent me home. I wanted to see the world, and this was a chance to do that. We traveled around playing different teams in different cities, and our goal was to "get souls for the Lord."

As we were learning all about how to save others, I grew more and more unsure. We were to tell our Christian story—some call it their testimony—to the team we were playing during halftime. When it was my turn, my sweaty red face hid my nerves, but the guilt swelled inside of me. *Oh God, I'm about to be caught*, I thought. They would realize I didn't have a story, so I made one up. It was good too. It was poetic and beautiful and about God's love and presence in my life—all of which was true—but then I said there was this one moment when I decided Jesus was the only way for me and that I asked him into my heart—not true. I convinced everyone I had been saved to avoid being saved.

I was a master chameleon who knew enough Bible verses to get by. Honesty meant less to me than acceptance at the time. The discomfort of lying was there, but the risk of not being a part of the group? Well, that just couldn't happen.

As a Catholic, I was never taught the Bible the way my peers were. Most of them were raised in a Baptist church where reciting verses was a part of their upbringing. Being Catholic in Mississippi was weird. I hadn't memorized verses or tried to save others from their sins by convincing them that accepting Jesus into their heart was their only way to salvation. That idea was foreign to me.

It wasn't until Athletes in Action and FCA came into my life that I began wanting to understand what this "saving" business was about. None of it made sense to me deep down. In fact, it made me terribly uncomfortable. I didn't come into the world thinking there was anything wrong with me and I needed to be fixed. I learned through church, more than anywhere else, that I was broken, a sinner, and that my worthiness was tied to others' opinions, ideas, and beliefs.

Being "saved," to me, was a label I could put on myself in order to deem myself worthy again. I wanted to fully grasp what it meant, so I explored the concept further so I could understand Southern culture and my friends more. The people around me believed life was only worth living if they were in the right religious standing, although they refused to call their belief system a "religion." As far as I could tell, unless you were "saved," you were doomed to hell since heaven was reserved only for those who were righteous enough to accept Jesus into their hearts—whatever that means. I was hoping it could be the answer to what I thought I was lacking from the Catholic Church. It wasn't.

I had the opportunity to tour because I was on the Mississippi State basketball team. In fact, it was during one of our practices that Athletes in Action came to tell us about what they were doing around the world. One of my teammates went on the second tour with me after I convinced her it was worth it.

I was the spiritual leader of the team. Nobody ever said it out loud, but the coaches made it very clear by asking me to run team Bible studies and constantly calling me into their offices to help them reach teammates who had gone "off course." I didn't get much playing time, but there were high expectations of me to keep everyone morally on track and keep the team together.

One of my coaches would often call me to talk about my other teammates. She would ask me to come into her office so we could talk.

It made me nervous to walk into any of my coaches' offices. My future hung in their hands. I was on scholarship, but there's no security in that. My ride was always being threatened by newer recruits. I did what I was told, improving dramatically at my three-point shot and becoming as strong at handling the ball with my left hand as my right, but it never seemed to be enough.

One of my coaches was sitting behind her desk when I walked in one day. I sat in a chair on the other side of her desk and was grateful for the barrier between us. While my feelings for her were complicated, I looked up to her and wanted her approval.

When she looked at me, it felt like she was seeing right through me. This time was no different. "Tell me about what is going on with Sarah. I've noticed she has a special relationship with someone back home, and I don't think it is serving her best interests."

My heart sank because I knew what was coming. "I'm not sure, Coach. I know she isn't doing well, but I don't know if that's why."

Coach kept hinting, "I think your teammate could really use your leadership and guidance in this situation. Why don't you get her to go on the next AIA tour with you? Maybe together, we could help her get God in her life."

I shifted in my seat with angst swirling in my belly. Changing others wasn't my forte, but my inner voice wasn't important enough to listen to yet. "Sure. I can help with that." Maybe joining forces with Coach would earn me more playing time. We all knew my teammate was dating a woman. In college sports, at the time, if you were gay, you couldn't talk about it, and no one could know about it outside of the team—especially any major donors.

Sarah and I were good friends, so I did end up asking her to go overseas with me during my second tour to play basketball and spread the gospel. I even helped her raise the money to do so. Surely that would cure her.

We both left for our summer travels excited to meet new people. Once we arrived, I tried to keep my distance from Sarah to avoid the guilt that lingered in the air when she was near me. While I had agreed to take her on the trip for the sake of guiding her to inner peace, no one else knew my motives, so I rewrote the agenda.

Just when I thought I was free from the pressure of others' expectations, the weight crushed me in an unexpected interaction with a stranger. We were in Poland walking home from dinner after a game. One of the Polish players and I were vibing. It wasn't a Christian talk; it was a God talk. Authentic and safe. She wasn't Christian, but I thought I was, so I said what came naturally to me. I wasn't trying to convince her of anything. I just asked her questions, which she reciprocated—questions about life, questions about God's existence and the purpose of our own, questions about the turmoil in the world and what we could do to alleviate it.

As our walk back to our hostel was coming to an end, I could see my teammates eyeing me and whispering to one another.

They bolted inside to leave us alone. It was time for me to convince this Polish woman to ask Jesus into her heart. That was our mission, after all. I had never been so nervous in my life, but I knew I had to try. The acceptance of the group outweighed the loud voice inside of me that was saying, *You can't force beliefs on another person.* There I was, about to turn this incredible connection into a religious project and try to convince this woman I had the answers to her path to heaven. I wanted to hug her and bolt. But I didn't.

I asked my new friend, "Would you pray with me?"

She backed off and crossed her arms, "Yes, but I don't understand what we are praying for." The trust we'd built gave me the confidence to proceed. I grabbed her hands and closed my eyes. I could feel her staring at me. Before I became a part of Athletes in Action, I didn't even know how to pray out loud. Prayer had been something reserved for me in my heart and with God. Before, it was sacred. Right then, I made it unholy.

I prayed, "God, thank you for this conversation and my new friend. Please help her accept Jesus into her heart." I looked up to find her even more confused, so I said, "Are you ready to accept Jesus into your heart?"

"I don't know what that means." She stretched her arms out toward me and waved her hands back and forth. "I am uncomfortable saying yes."

I bowed my head again and prayed anyway, "Jesus, please enter this woman's heart. Amen." What I really meant was that she wasn't good enough as she was and needed to go through this process for her "sins" to be forgiven. She had to pray with me and accept Jesus to be worthy.

She slipped her hands out of mine, and I took a step backward. I had just violated her trust in me, and I knew it. Her eyes shifted back and forth while she searched for something to say, but she didn't say anything. She turned around and walked away instead.

When I turned to walk into the hostel, all my teammates were there waiting to ask me if she had prayed with me. I said yes, which was technically true, but they were under the impression I had just saved this woman from damnation. They were ecstatic. There, I had done it again. I earned their favor. I earned their acceptance. I'd performed like I was trained to, and I was never going to do that again.

The Polish woman showed a lot of grace after our praying encounter. She acted as though it didn't happen, and we continued to grow a friendship. We were pen pals for years to come, and we wrote so many great letters talking about our lives and what we were up to. We talked more about God, life, and all the things we discussed in our initial conversation. I remained friends with her longer than any of my teammates from that basketball tour overseas.

During that same tour, there were two teammates who had gotten so close, the team questioned their relationship with one another. Were they more than friends? It was the impression we all got. There were talks of sending them home. We all judged from afar and with one another, unconcerned about that verse in our holy book that told us not to judge unless we wanted to be judged the same way. After determining what they were up to with no evidence, we finally confronted them. The women were crushed. They couldn't believe we were deeming them gay before asking for the truth. They denied any type of romantic relationship. We had our answer, but the damage was done. We'd broken their trust. We made it our business when it wasn't our business, and we'd judged when we certainly lacked the credentials to do so.

Once again, the Christian high horse rode in and destroyed a relationship in the name of salvation. We couldn't see that appreciating our lives and all the wonders in them (love, trust, friendship) were as important as the next life. Their vision of eternal life, for themselves and everyone else, was the driving force behind every decision. I was beginning to see just how convinced and how caught up I had become in not honoring my own truth. I could see all the damage happening in and around me, and I was a part of it.

I didn't go on a third tour. My soul couldn't handle it.

Sarah was different when we returned home too. Her journey overseas definitely changed her. I am not sure whether for better or worse, but she broke up with the woman she'd been dating when we got back. I don't know the driving force behind her decision, but I know she had seen how the other two women were treated when they were questioned about their relationship.

After I came out, Sarah was livid with me. She left me one of the most hateful voicemails I have ever received. I can't even repeat the words. But I don't blame her now. I see that she saw me as a hypocrite, and I certainly appeared so in a lot of ways. She trusted me to take her overseas, and she was exposed to people who saw a big part of her identity as an inherent evil. I didn't speak against their beliefs, as I was truly unsure of how I felt. I loved my gay friends, but I also saw how they were treated, so I wanted to keep my distance.

It would be two years between our trip overseas and when I came out. I lived a lifetime of change in those two years.

For one, I quit the basketball team. College basketball at an SEC school was my dream, and I gave it up because I didn't feel like I was being respected. I didn't like the pressure of being expected to be so much for everyone else yet not feeling respected enough by my coach to give me a chance on the court. I was a great player, and I deserved opportunities. I worked harder than anyone else on the team and put in the most hours. Every day in the summer, I was either on the track, in the weight room, or on the basketball court getting my shots in while everyone else was on break.

I also came to realize that changing other people for my coach wasn't my job. It made me uncomfortable. I switched over to playing softball and had the time of my life.

Not only did the softball coach respect me but he actually gave me a chance. I became a National Strength and Conditioning All-American under his leadership, batted over .300

each year, and was a solid defensive player. He allowed me to work my way into a starting role, and I never looked back. He was the first coach I ever had who didn't put pressure on me to be everyone else's support. I got to lead how I wanted to lead. My confidence was on the rise.

CHAPTER 5

I had never imagined myself kissing a girl.

During my first year of softball, I had been dating a guy for several years. Just before I turned twenty-one, we broke up. I assumed it was because I wouldn't have sex with him. Soon after we broke up, I became infatuated with one of my roommates. I always wanted to be around her. It wasn't my first infatuation with a woman, but while I was comfortable with having crushes, I was not comfortable acting on them.

One night after practice, as we were lying in my bed talking, bravery took over, and I leaned in and kissed her. She met me there, which was a relief. It was unlike anything I had ever felt. Something clicked. This was how it was supposed to feel. I suddenly belonged. I had found where my soul fit, but my environment hadn't caught up yet.

The exhaustion of keeping our relationship a secret was unsustainable, but I just couldn't fathom other people finding out that I was dating a woman. She was out but agreed to not tell people about me. She knew how hard it would be for me to come out in my hometown.

It was especially exhausting hiding from our other roommate who was straight and very Christian, and who I feared would not approve.

My girlfriend and I were able to hide for almost a year before people started finding out about us.

Our year of secrecy was lonely and agonizing. I felt the pull of deceit and shame in my stomach. I performed well as a student and an athlete and had finally found a part of myself that made sense, but all of that was clouded by uncertainty.

I started writing to channel my feelings and thoughts. Every journal entry started with "Dear God." I'd begin by asking for help with my spiritual, emotional, and mental tug-of-war.

This was the year before my entire world was rocked with both outward discrimination and defeating self-judgment. It was the year I was still me to everyone around me, when everyone still thought I was the same old Meagan: straight, Christian, and mentally strong. But I wasn't. I wasn't straight; I was questioning everything I had ever learned about Christianity; and my mental toughness was a facade. I began to drift away from my Christian friends and distance myself from my gay friends. I didn't want either to catch on to who I was becoming. Each day, I was susceptible to being found out, so I had to tread carefully. I was afraid of the future but yearned to be seen for who I was. I was also caught up in my label defining me, which isn't a bad thing if you accept what your labels are.

On the softball field, I had an amazing year. Hiding my true self somehow motivated me to be a better softball player. If I could be my best on the field, maybe no one would notice I was gay. I worked hard inside and outside of practice and played with more confidence as a result. I made plays in the outfield that only practice and complete surrender in the moment could materialize. We practiced diving catches every day, but the ones I made when it really counted were beyond comprehension.

After a game, my softball coach announced in front of the team I had just received the National Strength and Conditioning All-American award. My strength coach had submitted my name. I had no clue that such an award existed, which made the moment so rewarding for me. I was being seen for who I was without knowing anyone was paying that much attention. The award wasn't about how I performed or played. It was about the payoff of giving my all to something I cared about. I was finally feeling the freedom of trusting something bigger than myself in a way I never had before. I understood that if I did my best and allowed myself to let go of moments of doubt on the field, I was always more capable than when I tried to control those moments. Although I hadn't come out of the closet yet, things were beginning to click. I was building an internal space that would get me through the coming years.

I was beginning to see who I could be. I could be gay and close to God, and I was experiencing new dimensions of that closeness through my pen and paper. I was journaling my heart's cravings, and as a result, I stopped reaching for the God outside of me and could finally hear the God within me saying, "I love you." The moments of clarity were subtle and rare, but they brought me temporary peace. I was starting to experience what it was like to become my own haven.

This, of course, all happened without any negative outside influence pressuring me to be perfect or judging me for being gay. I hadn't come out of the closet yet. I wasn't sure if I was ready. While not being out yet felt like a prison in some ways, I was starting to feel free.

That freedom all slipped away when my ex-boyfriend outed me and an onslaught ensued. I felt strong in some moments, but not in many. I became defensive to protect myself. I was panicking on the outside and clinging to any safety I felt in my bedroom with my pen and paper. It was the only place I could completely be myself and feel understood.

Other people constantly challenged me and my motives. Strangers demanded, "Do you know your spiritual Daddy?" Their eyes pierced mine as they prepared to pounce at any sign of irresolution. These questions took me aback every time, but I never hesitated. I knew God. I knew the deep, still voice within me and around my heart.

After coming out, a year passed before I would leave Mississippi and move to Tallahassee, Florida. It was a year of turmoil for me, a year of questioning everything and everyone. I didn't trust many people to love me for me. Not only had my time ended in playing sports in college but I was also finishing up graduate school and trying to decide what I wanted my life to be like. Leaving Mississippi meant leaving a dark fog. I could finally start over again and be who I was meant to be.

I broke up with my first girlfriend after a year of dating. The pressure of being in a relationship with someone while dealing with all the people who were questioning me was too overwhelming. I needed time to figure things out.

After the breakup, I was reeling with sadness and needed a source of comfort. I decided to go to my parents' house. I was sitting on a barstool in the kitchen, trying to stuff my feelings deep into my stomach, when my mom approached me and laid down a stack of papers.

"I looked up some ways to help you."

I stared at the papers in front of me. They were about a camp that would "turn me back" to being heterosexual. Tears were making their way to my eyes when I reached the point of no return. I couldn't remain speechless anymore.

"I don't want to be fixed!"

She looked like a deer in headlights, upset that I was upset. "You've just been so unhappy. I want to help you."

She had mistaken my brokenness as a call for help when all I needed was to be held and accepted.

I got up, snatched the papers out of her hand, and left the house.

I thought about my mom on the drive back to my home. She was in the process of losing her best friend to lung cancer. The sadness she was already facing seemed unbearable, and the need to fix my mom's pain had always been something I had taken on. She never asked me to, but I did nonetheless. I never wanted her to be sad. In fact, from a young age, I often questioned if her sadness was because of something I did. It was one of the main reasons I made it a point to play by the rules. Now I know that I was just guessing about what her emotions meant. Since we didn't talk about things, I had no information or patterns to base my assumptions on. I didn't know how to talk. I only knew how to hold pain close to my chest.

It seemed as though she was afraid for me. Whether it was fear of how I was going to be treated in this life or where I was going to go when I died, I wasn't sure. But at the time, it just felt like rejection.

The unconditional love I'd always received from her suddenly felt conditional. I wasn't sure how to cope without her full-on acceptance. While sitting at my desk, I glanced at the papers she'd handed me earlier in the day, crumpled them up, and threw them in the trash.

Desperate for my mom to understand me, I decided to stop by my parents' office the next day. When I walked in, one of my professors was standing there. I was in Mississippi State's counselor education program at the time, and her class was my favorite. I was not expecting to see her. My mom was crying, and my professor was trying to comfort her. I hoped to God this wasn't an intervention.

I didn't know how my professor felt about me being gay yet, so I wasn't sure what to think or feel. I remained quiet.

My mom spoke up. "Dr. Wells is going to help us through this."

Her eyes were a comforting presence, so I welcomed the opportunity to have someone to talk to. I needed a lifeline, so maybe Dr. Wells could be that for me. She walked over to me and squeezed me tighter than I had been squeezed in weeks. I booked a session with her before she left, and so did my parents. We never went to counseling together, but we did all work with Dr. Wells.

My mom sought out additional help with their priest at the Catholic church I was raised in. I was never interested in seeking help from the church I grew up in because churches were no longer a place where I felt safe. When she was talking to the priest about her fears for me and how I was going to be treated, the priest told her, "Just imagine what Meagan has been through already. Imagine her tears."

When my mom shared that with me, she also revealed the priest's words caused her to break down in tears. She was so focused on others' perception of me that she hadn't realized the depth of my heartbreak. She was trying her best to understand something inside of me that she couldn't understand, and that was hard for her.

My parents were surrounded by people who were letting them have their experience without judgment, and I tried to surround myself with the same type of people. My mom was scared to share who I was to extended family members.

She allowed her fear to make her choices for her in the same ways I had before I told her I was gay.

I was extremely fortunate to have a few friends who I didn't feel judged by. They listened to me, let me cry, and became the only safe ground I had. They loved me beyond right and wrong. Most of my other friends said they loved me but didn't agree with my lifestyle. They were "loving the sinner, hating the sin," as they'd been instructed to. That statement always hurt and threw me into self-doubt and a lack of trust in the relationship.

When I went to counseling, I would sit in the counselor's office and cry for an hour. I was detached from myself and everything I had ever known, which was forcing me to find out who I really was. I had to break down any and all expectations I had of myself and get down to the dark, deep corners of my soul where I'd hidden all of my grief and doubts. My tears, faithful and honest, made a way. They shed light for the path and led me, one step at a time, to each day. And that's all I could muster . . . making it to the next day.

I think we all have moments like this in our lifes, moments when who we are and who we thought we were come into question. It's a reckoning of sorts, an opportunity to see ourselves in a new light that shines from within and not the light we see in others' eyes when they gaze on us out of their own satisfaction.

I had relied so much on what other people thought of me that once they thought so little of me, I had to find a way to rely on my own acceptance. But good God, how was I supposed to even begin that journey?

Every part of me wanted to hide, run, and get the hell out of Mississippi. My older brother's words, "Leave Mississippi, it'll be easier," constantly echoed between my ears.

I couldn't leave yet, but I could escape what was familiar. I started to hang out with people who didn't bring out the best in me. Something in me wanted to confirm to myself that I wasn't worthy of love and comfort anymore. I began drifting from the person I knew I was deep down and started to look for validation from the outside. The freedom I felt while still closeted didn't feel protective anymore. My sense of self was muddled, and subconsciously, I didn't think I deserved to be happy—not fully, anyway. I dated, but not well. I would go after women who wanted to hide as much as I did, the opposite of what I needed to begin the healing process.

As I was finishing up my graduate degree at Mississippi State, I started looking for an internship outside of Mississippi. I needed space.

I began my time in graduate school at Mississippi State intending to be a counselor and derailed that track when I realized that if I couldn't get myself together, then I couldn't be an efficient counselor. I switched to rehabilitation counseling so I could help people with disabilities get the services they needed to create a successful life for themselves. There was a part of me that needed to advocate for others since I didn't feel like I could advocate for myself.

I could have continued my studies at Mississippi State in the blindness and low-vision field, but I desperately wanted to leave. I found Florida State's program, applied, and received a full scholarship. Around the same time, I landed an amazing internship with the Americans with Disabilities Act governmental office in Tallahassee, where Florida State is. It felt like things were aligning for me to move on with my life.

I dove headfirst into making a way for myself.

When the day came for me to leave Starkville, I could breathe again. I no longer had to face each morning with isolation and sadness. I could go somewhere where no one knew me and start over. I could choose an authentic life from the beginning. I had no idea the challenges I'd face in my fight for authenticity.

CHAPTER 6

I had a major crush on one of my professors. Butterflies fluttered in my chest every time I saw her, and whenever she spoke to me, I never knew what to say back.

It wasn't just an infatuation. I had feelings for her.

Desiree was out of my league: tall, gorgeous, and straight. There were rumors going around about the man she was dating, that he worked at the university, but no one knew who he was.

I didn't take her class until my last semester at Florida State, but it was a small program so everyone knew everyone. Our interactions were minimal, but they were meaningful for me. There was something about the excitement of having a crush on someone who seemed unattainable that gave me energy. I was able to fill myself up with that and neglect the shame I carried from Mississippi.

The looming darkness of my coming out experience was inside of me somewhere, but I tried not to let it pull me in. I avoided my grief by staying busy enough with work, school, and rugby, my newfound hobby.

I dated throughout the year, but nothing ever lasted because I was scared to love again. I was scared to love at all.

The women I dated brought me down, and I seemed to be only interested in those who were unattainable. I clearly wasn't ready for anything serious, and because I was living alone for the first time in my life, I had time and space to explore other ways of thinking and seeing God.

I found a Catholic church that considered itself liberal. It had a gay Venezuelan priest. His hugs were the warmest, most accepting hugs—something I needed from someone in the church. They accepted me there, so much so that, eventually, they asked me to do a sermon. I had spoken to groups before as an athlete, and I loved speaking, but sharing myself in front of a spiritual community again? That was risky.

When I stood up in front of everyone, I was shaking. In the audience were my rugby friends staring back at me along with the other attendees, about ten people total. They emanated a warmth that I could feel at the podium. In the past, I had often read my speeches, but this time, I spoke from my heart. I talked about losing my friend, Kayln, and the impact it had on me. I had never processed it out loud in a group before. I wasn't ready to talk about being gay or my coming out experience, so I avoided that topic altogether. Instead, I focused on how important it is to appreciate life and those around us because we never know what will happen.

After the service, my friends gave me giant hugs and expressed how deeply touched they were. It was nice to be celebrated after sharing my heart. That moment confirmed how much I loved public speaking. Sharing my story was cathartic. I was becoming more of myself.

During the school year, I'd occasionally stop by Desiree's office to chat. We talked about the classes I was taking, which often led to conversations about more personal things. Each time I was there, I observed papers overflowing from every available surface and started drinking in inspirational quotes from authors on the wall that I had never heard of before. After each visit, I was drunk from her presence, and I wanted to understand why. I was grateful to Desiree for showing me a new way of thinking without knowing it. I started accumulating my own copies of the books I saw lying in her office.

There was one book in particular that caught my eye, *The Power of Now*, by Eckhart Tolle. Being an avid reader, I'd come across some mind-shifting books, but this one hit differently. The concept of living in the moment caught my attention, but what did that concept actually mean? Sure, I had lived in the moment before, but I didn't know it was something I could choose, especially all the time.

For the first time, I saw that I was in control of my perspective. That single realization has pulled me forward in many difficult moments over the years. Knowing that I get to choose my reactions and that I can accept the moment as it is are lessons I desperately needed to overcome my lack of self-worth. Although I didn't master staying in the present moment then, and I still haven't, I am more aware now than

I have ever been, and it all started with that one book, which led me to many others.

As I entered my final semester at Florida State, Desiree's class was the last one I took.

The class required a lot of time outdoors, as we were learning how to "be blind" by wearing blindfolds and using a long cane to make our way around a block, in and out of buildings, and across streets. We learned all the necessary skills to efficiently help our future vision-impaired clients.

My attraction to Desiree was all-consuming. I reveled in any ounce of attention she gave me. For one of my tests, I had to walk four different floors of a building on my own with Desiree. I could hear my heart pounding from the nervousness of not wanting to let her down. I couldn't imagine the electricity I felt around her was one-sided, considering the lingering touches on my arms or shoulders she'd give me each class.

I had to keep telling myself, *She's straight. She's my professor.* It was just a crush I never thought would turn into anything.

Once I officially finished the class, things changed. My group of straight friends decided they wanted to go to a gay bar with me to support me, and we invited Desiree. To my surprise, she decided to join us.

When she arrived, I felt confident enough to buy her a drink. She wanted top shelf vodka. I didn't hesitate, even though my bank account was dry. We spent the evening talking and flirting and eventually ended up on the dance floor together. All of my friends decided to leave, but Desiree wanted to stay with me. We danced until the bar closed. I walked her to her car, and we hugged for a long time, but I wasn't brave enough to try anything more.

After that night, we started texting a lot and having long phone calls. Before I knew it, I was in her house. We spent the evening learning from each other, and I was fascinated by her perspectives. She said she had never had such deep conversations with someone before. Just as the sun was beginning to rise, she invited me into her bedroom to sleep for a few hours before we both had to get up and go to work.

I was incredibly nervous. She asked me if I wanted a pair of sweatpants instead of my jeans, but I refused. I couldn't change in front of her. I was being awkward, lying on my back and trying not to look at her. She closed her eyes for a while, so I turned ever so often to look at her. Every time her breath shifted, I'd pretend I was asleep. I was exhausted, but my mind was racing. Eventually I turned over to face her, and there she was, looking back at me. I reached over and pulled her close to me, and we kissed.

We didn't tell a soul. Even though I wasn't her student anymore, no one could know. She didn't want anyone in the department to find out about us. I had to hide again.

I had already accepted a job in Miami and was leaving in a few short weeks, which gave little time for our relationship to establish any sort of foundation.

While I loved my first girlfriend at Mississippi State and other people along the way, I would say that Desiree was the first person I had truly fallen in love with.

I was so afraid the distance was going to keep us from moving forward in our relationship, but she kept putting in the effort, so I did too. We met in Orlando occasionally to see each other. She would fly down to see me, and I would fly back up to see her.

In Miami, I lived in a room in an older woman's apartment a few blocks from the beach on Key Biscayne. The woman was strange but kind. Those few months were incredible. I was just a fifteen-minute drive away from work in downtown Miami, and I was writing a lot. I had a heightened sense of everything. I would run to the beach every day after work and stare off into the sea, breathing in its expansiveness as if we were one. I'd then run back to the apartment, lift some weights, then sit in a rocking chair in the corner of my room and write quietly until Desiree called me in the evening. I began imagining myself as this big-time writer who spoke to large audiences—the same dream I had when I was younger, except at this point, it felt possible.

Before I knew it, I was using the work printer to print out my first book. It was a collection of essays about my spiritual journey from high school to college. I still wasn't ready to face coming out of the closet so publicly. I took the pages of the book, punched three holes in each page, and placed it into a large three ring binder. Once I was done, I closed the binder and beamed with pride. I shared it with my coworkers, and we bonded over some of my musings. I held on to the book my entire time in Miami, as I was unsure of how to begin the publishing process.

After just a few short months of being apart, Desiree decided to quit her job and move to be closer to me.

Once Desiree arrived, we moved to a new apartment in North Miami. It was a further drive to work and not within walking distance to the beach. Among all the changes, I didn't stop writing, but I did slow down. My life became very full, very quickly, mostly because I spent much of it stuck in traffic. I hated it. The freedom of my Key Biscayne apartment was no more. On top of that, my internship ended up turning into a full-time job, so I was slated to stay in Miami for a while. But all of it was tolerable because Desiree was there.

She and I found a church we wanted to try out called Unity on the Bay. We were welcomed and accepted and, for once, part of a majority. It was a surreal experience for me to see people celebrating being Christian and still being gay. Desiree and I were on the same page spiritually and politically. Things were starting to click for me spiritually. Immersing ourselves into a church where I could be myself was empowering.

Desiree moved in with me in October, and my parents came down for a visit the following spring. When I'd told them Desiree and I were moving in together, they were under the impression that we were just friends, and I needed a roommate to make rent work. I wanted to keep our relationship from them because I didn't want a repeat of the experience I had when I came out. We hadn't talked about me being gay or my dating life since I'd broken up with my first girlfriend, and I wasn't ready to. My parents probably weren't ready either.

They figured out Desiree was my girlfriend when they arrived and noticed they would be sleeping in one room and we would be sleeping in the other. No words were ever exchanged about our relationship. However, it felt like my parents were attempting to move forward and see me for me again. They were kind to Desiree and did everything they could to make her feel comfortable by engaging in conversation, asking about her family, and paying for our dinner, even though I am sure it was hard for them to completely accept our relationship.

While they were visiting, my parents and I went for a walk. Desiree had been offered a job in Colorado. She was going to take it, so I had to decide if I was going to follow. She didn't seem attached to me following her, which was a bit heartbreaking. She wanted me to make the decision for myself and not for her. Her reasoning seemed mature enough, but it just meant to me that she wasn't sure about us. The red flag was waving profusely in the wind, and I didn't notice it.

As I walked down the sidewalk in front of our apartment complex with my parents, I got up the guts to tell them, "Desiree got a job in Colorado, and I am thinking about going."

They were perplexed since I had only been in my full-time job for a few months. There was an awkward silence for a few moments before my mom chimed in, "Do you have a job lined up there?"

My body sank with relief when her first question wasn't a hard one. "No, not yet. But I am not worried about that. I feel like, deep down, this is what I want to do."

Everyone's energy shifted from discomfort to ease when my mom said, "Well, sweetheart, you need to follow your heart."

I was excited about the opportunity to move somewhere new and the fact that my parents were behind my decision. We started talking about all the things we would do in Colorado when they came to visit. When they left Miami to go back to Mississippi, even though we didn't talk about anything related to my sexuality, I felt a surge of acceptance between us that I hadn't experienced since before coming out.

Desiree and I didn't tell anyone in our department from Florida State about our relationship. She did tell some of her colleagues and good friends who were in other departments. Being that she was over ten years older than me, I expected her to take the lead on how open we would be. It was hard for me to place my own confidence in someone else's hands. I wanted to be out in the open, but she wasn't completely ready for that. She didn't want to tell her family, yet at the same time, she seemed proud when she would introduce me to the new people we met together. That made me feel safe and secure in a lot of ways. It also meant I didn't have to be the one telling people. I preferred that.

For a long time, Desiree was sure her family would disown her. Later on, she told her little sister, who ended up being very supportive and loving to me. Still, she hid me from most of her family, but she was open with new people about our relationship. This inconsistency and complexity made me feel like she was incapable of loving me the way I needed to be loved. I was tired of hiding.

I wanted to be myself in the world and was progressing toward self acceptance. However, I still had deep-seated shame about who I was. My spiritual life was expanding along with my worldview, and Desiree had a lot to do with that. I was beginning to see the world as a place where my dreams could come true. I just didn't know what it was going to take to get there.

I had this innocent and pure perspective that it would be easy to become a best-selling author. I miss that perspective. It was hopeful and faithful and trusting. I didn't know life was about to get extremely challenging and that I was going to have to learn to start truly loving myself to get through the next phase.

CHAPTER 7

Desiree broke up with me over Gmail chat.

I was at work and did a double take at the computer screen. I couldn't believe what I was reading. Everything went blurry before my feelings had a chance to catch up.

I had just changed jobs and was being trained to manage a local Comfort Keepers—a company that provides in-home care for people who can't fully care for themselves. I never liked working for other people, but I didn't see another way for myself at the time. When I got that message from Desiree, I sobbed and panicked and left for the day. I'm lucky they didn't fire me for that. I was devastated. It was an inconsolable despair like I have never felt before and will never feel again—not like that.

After a year of living in turmoil together in Colorado, she did the right thing because I didn't have the strength to do it myself.

At that time in my life, I had no sense of self. I thought I did, but I didn't. I had no inner strength and had no confidence

I could make it in Colorado without her. I allowed her to fill the part of me that was empty. When she left me empty again, I needed to love myself. Instead, I fell apart.

Our struggles began before we moved to Colorado, but I was determined to make the relationship work anyway. The "newness" of the first six months there gave us a renewed excitement for life, and there was so much exploring to do that we stayed busy and happy. She traveled home with me for my older brother's wedding, and while all the children adored her, I noticed her interactions with other adults were minimal. She claimed that she was uncomfortable. Distance began to grow between us. At home in Colorado, she was spending longer hours working while I was self-deprecating, feeling completely insecure because of her lack of attention.

Several months later, when we went to Mississippi for Christmas, she spent most of her time in our room at my parent's house. My family had opened their hearts and home to her during the most celebrated and cherished holiday of the year, and she was locked upstairs on her computer. My family went overboard to make her feel comfortable. They all bought her presents and treated her like everyone else, but her shutting them out was a preview of what was happening to me.

Once we returned to Colorado, things kept getting harder for us, as the distance between Desiree and I was becoming almost impossible to bridge. What was worse, I couldn't talk to her. I was afraid of her temper. I would passive aggressively make comments instead, which sent her over the edge. We were fighting all the time, and our intimacy disappeared. Our fights got so bad that once, I threw a bag of dog food down a flight of stairs because she purposely chose to cut me with her words. A flare went off in my chest, and that was the only response I could muster. I scared the dogs and made Desiree even angrier.

I was becoming someone I didn't like.

When my family came to visit us in the spring, it was clear to them that something was off. I was torn between spending time with them or Desiree because she wouldn't interact with them. I had to practically beg her to go to dinner with us. She seemed miserable. I certainly was. I had put my identity into our relationship and thought it was going to be forever. She made me feel like I was "the one," and I certainly thought she was "the one," but as things fell apart, I didn't know how to communicate what I was feeling, much less how to fix it. She wouldn't give me anything—just anger. The freedom I had been so excited about was absent again. I felt stuck, lost, confused, like I'd misread everything. I couldn't trust her judgment or mine. I wasn't sure what was real anymore.

All wasn't lost during my parents' visit. That week, I learned a publisher wanted to print a book I'd just written, *Creating Your Heaven on Earth*. The feeling of this triumph against the pain of my relationship felt like two different worlds.

I'd written a book before but tucked it away after receiving some helpful feedback that it wasn't ready for publication. During my initial months in Colorado, I was discovering so much about my spirituality that I wanted to give it a voice. I wanted to proclaim what I knew to be true. It was like a new portal was opening up inside me, so I spent my evenings writing in the basement to capture all the newness I was birthing. I even created a vision board that said, "*Creating Your Heaven on Earth*: New York Times Best Seller." I believed in that book so much that I submitted hundreds of inquiries. Eventually, I got a yes.

When I got the email, I showed it to my parents right away. We were all in the living room together, except for Desiree, who was downstairs in the basement working. I ran downstairs to share the news with her. "Hey, guess what? A publisher just emailed me, and they want to publish my book!"

She seemed hollow. I wasn't sure if she had heard me, so I repeated myself. She looked up from her computer with vitriol in her eyes. "Did you tell your family before you told me?"

Like an abused puppy who didn't want to upset their owner, I responded, "Yes, but they were right there when I opened the email."

"Who cares! I've been the one supporting you this whole time. I can't believe you wouldn't tell me first!" she argued.

I felt lower than I did that day in the chapel when my ministry leader tried to pray the sin out of me. Desiree knew how important it was to me to become a published writer, but her reaction soured the excitement I'd waited so long for.

The rest of the week was torturous. Desiree went off to travel for work, and I barely heard from her while she was gone. It was then I wondered if she'd started a relationship with someone else. Our relationship was on a path to nowhere, and it would take four more months of agony before we would break it off. I lost around twenty pounds during that time. I couldn't eat.

I suspected Desiree was cheating on me when I saw texts on her phone from guys I didn't know. Every time I confronted her about it, she blew up. There was no way we were going to get through it. I ran to my spirituality for answers and read a quote in a magazine that helped shift my perspective a bit. It read something like this: "Everything is God. You choose how you want to see the world around you." Instantly, I was transported to a world where Desiree's waves of moodiness didn't even phase me. She saw the shift in me, too, and became gentler. I was only able to maintain that state of being for about thirty minutes, but it was a significant moment that showed me what I was capable of. I will forever remember that moment of being outside of my body and seeing life and others as they truly are.

After our breakup, we still had to live together while I found another place to stay. We slept in separate rooms. I offered to go to counseling to see if we could work things out. She refused. As she was preparing to go out of the country for work, we did have one last meaningful conversation. Oddly enough, we were getting along after the breakup. It was a weird and painful time, but at least we were beginning to talk. We interacted as friends and did our own separate things as roommates.

When I asked her if she was sure ending our relationship was what she wanted, she sighed, "Yes, it's just too much love for me. Your family, you, I just can't handle all of the love." A jolt of understanding ran through my veins. She was as insecure, if not more, as I was. Everything suddenly made sense. She was reflecting to me how I felt about myself.

I found a place to stay with a good friend who gave me no deadline. My mom came out to help me move my things once Desiree left to go out of the country. I will never forget sharing a bed with my mom. I was crying, she was holding me, and my pup, Roxy, was curled around my feet. She had held me like that when I was little and I was asking her hard questions. This breakup was forcing me to deal with the trauma of coming out so many years before. I could tell that my pain was pulling at my mom, as she couldn't help her own tears from falling. I don't know what I would have done if she hadn't come to get me through that transition.

My pain forced my mom to finally tell her family I was gay. They all wanted to know how I was doing, and she wanted to be honest. She also knew that I mentioned in my book I was gay, so she felt like she had to tell everyone before they read the news for themselves. She did it out of protection for me.

I was changing little by little, tear by tear. I cried everywhere I went: at church, with friends, in the car, in bed alone with Roxy. There seemed to be an endless supply of tears. The hurt was made of shame and loneliness and an unknowing of what my future would be.

To deal with my loneliness, I began to write again while I waited for my publisher to put the finishing touches on *Creating Your Heaven on Earth*. I started writing a new book, *It Is What It Is*, and started taking classes at the church I was attending. Desiree stopped going to that church after our breakup, and I went more often. The people there embraced me and helped me get through the split. I was surrounded by amazing people. The friends I met through that church are still my friends after all these years. I began reaching out and asking others to be in my life because I knew I needed to let people in to cure my sadness. As time went on, things got easier.

I started gaining weight again and eating normally. I even started exercising. Roxy and I did a lot of hiking. Our favorite place was Horsetooth Reservoir. We'd climb down some of its steep cliffs all the way to the water where Roxy could swim. It was one place I could go to be completely alone. It was there where I started talking to God and actually listening to what was within me.

It was time for me to start creating my own heaven on earth, which meant letting go of the ideals I had learned about God growing up. I was ready to move on from all of my beliefs attached to Christianity and find a way of thinking about and viewing the world that worked for me. And that's what I set out to do. I had no idea how challenging it would be.

CHAPTER 8

I decided to have sex with a man.

It wasn't calculated. It started innocently enough with a visit from a friend. But as our evening of catching up over drinks progressed, there was a shift. His hand lingered on mine. I lifted my eyes to his as he lightly traced a pattern over the back of my hand. He wasn't what I wanted, but *it* was: intimacy. I longed to be seen, to be validated. My skin prickled as the yearning for connection became palpable. His touch led to a kiss. Our kiss led to sex.

Nothing about it felt right. If I ever needed confirmation I was gay, that was it.

I started talking to a few women, but nothing panned out. I certainly wasn't healed from my Desiree experience, but I needed to start over and find the intimate connection I desperately wanted.

I was rushing to fill myself back up instead of carefully connecting to my spiritual essence. I kept looking for someone to be in love with. I had lost touch with my connection to God, which was crushed by everyone else's perception of me when I was forced out of the closet. The backlash of loving my first girlfriend led me to question the God in my heart, and loving Desiree led me to doubt everything about myself.

As my life seemed to spiral out of control, I began to get impatient with people who couldn't accept me for who I was—especially my family.

My mom was one of those people. After my breakup with Desiree, it seemed that my mom was hoping I was going to be "less gay." She made a remark over the phone to me one day, something insinuating that my "phase" was coming to an end.

"Are you sure this is the life you want to live? Are you sure you can do it?"

Her comment took me back to the moment she handed me the conversion therapy papers. I was surprised this was coming from my mom, who had made such a genuine attempt to connect with Desiree and had supported me moving to Colorado with her. A whiplash back in time wasn't what I was expecting.

I bit back at her. "I don't understand why you can't move on and accept me." My hands were shaking as I was trying to hold onto the phone and pay attention to the road.

"Meagan, if you want me to accept you, then you have to be willing to accept me where I am too. I just want you to be happy, and you are miserable."

As hard as it was to hear, her honesty was what I needed. She was trying, putting herself out there, but it was a process that needed time and my patience. I backed off. I am so fortunate to have a mom who is open to having hard conversations. She has always been willing to love me despite not fully understanding me.

Through the classes I was taking at church, my work, the continued conversations with my mom, and my supportive friends, I was beginning to see that I could create the life I wanted. I was beginning to see what kind of love I wanted in my life and knew I deserved. My lack of confidence was still present, but the lack was slowly falling away.

During my transformation phase, there was a day I was felt the need to cry, so Roxy and I went up to Horsetooth Reservoir. We trekked to the water's edge. I looked over at Roxy, who was sitting on a rock with her eyes closed, facing the sun, and letting the wind hit her face. Tears of desperation and loneliness streamed down my own.

From the depths of my soul, I screamed out to the Universe: "I want to be loved the way that I love!"

I said it from that deep place reserved for the rare dreams we come to this earth to see miraculously come to fruition. It was a calling forth from my soul to find what it needed. It was letting go of knowing I couldn't do it alone. Suddenly, faith returned to me. I had been holding everything so tightly for so many years. I wanted God in my life but wouldn't let God in enough to trust I was worthy of any sort of happy life.

I wanted inner peace, but it was clear I couldn't do it on my own. I was looking for a partner, but more than that, I was looking for myself.

Several weeks later, I walked into my first meditation class, and there she was—Clare.

She had on slouchy green trousers, a black T-shirt, and a zip-up hoodie. Her hair was shaggy, and her beautiful blue eyes stared at me as I sat across the room from her. I was drawn to her ease. During meditations, I would often peek at her only to find her in a deep stillness—one that could not be moved. Her connection to her God was serene. I wanted that type of trust in God again.

Clare and I became fast friends. We often met up at church and sat together. After a service one Sunday, we were talking with some friends when she asked me my age. She gasped, her jaw dropping at the revelation that I was twenty-seven. With wide eyes, she said, "Well, I guess we can never date."

I hadn't thought about dating her, but when she said that, I realized I had a little crush on her. I wasn't in a hurry to start a relationship with anyone. I was still reeling from my breakup, and I didn't expect God to send someone so quickly. I was finally being given what I deserved, but all I did was resist. "So how old are you?"

Clare bent over laughing as she could barely get out her words. "Forty-two!" She was straight—available and wonderful, but straight. And old.

I didn't see any hope in dating a woman fifteen years older than me, so I let the thought go, but my feelings didn't go anywhere.

One evening during a break in class, I got up to look at the books on the shelves in our classroom. Everyone had left to go out into the hallway for a break, except Clare. As she got up, she walked behind me, grabbed my butt, and said, "You have a nice ass."

I froze as my face turned beet-red. As a Southern girl, I was reserved, and gay, so I was taken completely by surprise. I slowly turned around to find Clare uncertain of her actions as she quickly apologized and walked out of the room. As she was leaving the room, courage leapt up from my throat. "So, when are we going out?"

I could hear her laughing shyly as she scurried down the hallway with her back turned to me.

We didn't go out for a while, but we were forming a bond. As our friendship developed, Clare's presence in my life helped me begin to look at myself in a new way. I started seeing that I could change my own beliefs, but first I had to recognize what they were. While I believed deeply in myself and my writing, there were still beliefs about making it a career that I needed to dig into and redefine. I started that transformation by taking a look back at the messages I had received from my parents.

One day, back in college, I stood in the office of my dad's used car business talking to my parents. When I walked in the door, I could smell the perfume of a customer who had just left. With hints of lavender permeating the air, I looked up the short set of stairs to find my mom there helping my dad. It was just after my freshman year of college, and I was going to need to decide on a major soon. I was seeking out their advice on what they thought would be a reasonable choice.

When I was able to capture both of their attention between phone calls, keys clacking, and my dad rolling over the next deal in his mind, I told my parents I wanted to be a writer.

My dad blurted out, "What are you going to do to make money?"

I didn't respond. I just shook my head. In the wake of deflated hopes, my response was to choose a major, educational psychology, and chalk my writing up to a hobby. I didn't know any writers who were able to make a living doing it. I still had dreams, but I knew I had to pay the bills.

The harder life became, the more solace I found in writing. That's why I pushed relentlessly to make something of it after I finished college and started working in the real world. I knew there was no job that would ever fulfill me the way writing and speaking would.

My first book was to be published in November 2008. The independent press I signed with hired a marketer and covered all publishing and distribution costs. However, if I was going to travel, I had to pay my own way. My $28,000 per year job wasn't going to take me far, but I was going to do what I needed to do to forge my own path. I started with local book signings and traveled to places where I knew I had a following, like Tallahassee and Starkville. The church I was attending in Fort Collins also agreed to do a special signing for me.

Clare and I had been talking for a bit by then, but we hadn't gone out. While I was sitting and signing books at the end of the service, I saw her out of the corner of my eye. My feelings for her were clearly growing, because as she approached me I tried not to make eye contact. I wasn't ready to be seen.

Her overly optimistic energy was contagious, but I wasn't sure what to do with it yet. She bent down to hug me and said, "I want a book." I grabbed the next one in the stack and tried to hide the fact that my hands were shaking. My vision blurred as I grabbed the pen and started writing. After I signed her book, I was embarrassed that my handwriting looked like a five-year-old's.

After the signing, a bunch of friends decided to take me to lunch to celebrate. Clare said she wanted to ride with me. When she hopped in my gray 4Runner, she leaned back, put her right elbow on the arm rest, cocked her head to the right, looked at me and said, "I want to know everything about you. What's your story?"

No one had ever said that to me before. I've never been one to open up unless someone asked a question or invited me to speak. I am a little more outgoing and confident now, but at the time, that question was big. Did she really want to know everything? Yes, she did. She meant it. I would end up telling her everything as I slowly put my heart into her hands.

We couldn't get enough of each other after that. We were constantly texting, chatting, and emailing each other throughout our workdays.

I asked her to meet me for coffee on my lunch break in the middle of the week. Something special was happening between us, and I wanted to see her as much as possible. We chatted for hours until I realized I had been away from work too long and had to rush off. I texted her right away to ask her to join me for dinner.

After the workday, I walked outside of my basement office to find a dark, brisk evening. Snow threatened to feather from the clouds and dust the roads. I zipped my coat and met Clare at a restaurant near my office.

We sat down in a booth and quietly stared at each other. I couldn't get enough of looking at her and feeling like she could see me for who I was. She understood me and accepted me. With every distracting interruption, like our food being delivered to us or our glasses being refilled with water, we'd catch ourselves coming right back to one another's eyes. I found myself in her, but not in an unhealthy way—in a way that made sense to me. She'd require me to take care of myself and love myself, which I somehow knew.

With our coats and gloves on, we walked outside together into the snow, our warm hands clasped in the cold air. The soft crunch of the fresh snow lingered while we remained silent, unsure of what to say next. I paused to give her a hug. My right cheek sat next to hers for many moments before they glided past one another and we connected for our first kiss.

It was different from any other kiss. It was certain and confident. It was love, but not a love that would fill me up like all the others. It was a love that would gently guide me to loving myself.

Our age difference was hard for me to grasp and was one of the reasons I was hesitant to start a relationship with her. I was beginning my journey in the career I wanted, and I had just ended things with Desiree. Yet in all my vulnerability, Clare was patient and kind and graceful.

I know I hurt her a few times when I became distant or detached. I had never poured my heart out to anyone the way I did with her. She made me feel safe, loved, and accepted. That was new for me. And it was scary. Why is it that we are so afraid of being fully loved by someone? I had asked God to send me someone to love me the way that I loved, and here was someone who was love personified . . . and I was terrified.

It wasn't until the spring when I eventually said I wanted to make things official between us, and that was because some guy had asked her out. Just a hint of someone else being interested in her was all I needed to realize she was the one for me.

"Tell him you have a girlfriend," I said.

She looked at me, surprised, and responded, "Really?"

The thought of life without her was daunting. She was patient with me and gave me a chance to catch up to the idea that this was a commitment I wasn't going to take lightly. I didn't just want another relationship; I wanted to be sure I'd found my person. I wasn't up for the runaround again. My heart and soul couldn't take it.

CHAPTER 9

Once Clare was in my life, I had emotional support in a way I never had before. She believed in my dreams more than I did, which pushed me to places I wouldn't have gone on my own.

My publisher and publicist were able to book quite a few events for me. In between radio interviews and magazine articles, there were opportunities for speaking engagements and book signings all over the country. There was a part of me that expected great things to happen and another part of me that was in disbelief my first book was having such success. Each time I received an email with another invitation, I'd quickly find a way to take them up on it.

The excitement made me want to quit my job, but the money wasn't rolling in yet. Although I had to pay all the expenses, I wasn't willing to say no to an opportunity. I had to find a way to make it all work. I was still living in my friend's house, and she was kind enough to not require any rent from me. Instead, I'd help take care of her sons and do work around the house. That enabled me to travel.

My first book signing in a city where no one knew me was in Skaneateles, New York. A woman who had a popular book club reached out to my publisher and wanted me to give a talk.

I, of course, said yes, even though it meant I had to pay for all costs associated with the trip. I coordinated with my publisher to meet him in New York City afterward and put together a small event with people I knew who lived there. My itinerary required me to fly from Denver to Pittsburgh, and then from Pittsburgh to Syracuse. I had an early flight to catch on the day of the book signing, which was scheduled for 6:30 that evening. I barely made the 30-minute check-in cut-off and had to run to my gate. Just in time, I narrowly squeezed through a crowd of people before the flight attendant shut the door.

The flight went smoothly. I was so full of anticipation and excitement, the exhaustion didn't matter to me. I was going across the country to sign books for people who didn't know me!

When I arrived in Pittsburgh, I rushed to the "departure" board to check on the gate assignment for my next flight, but I was cutting it close for that flight as well. When I found my flight, "CANCELED" in bright red letters stared back at me. My heart sank. I started to panic, so I called Clare to calm me down.

"Meagan, take a deep breath. Everything is going to be okay. Just trust whatever happens," she assured me.

Something shifted into a deep knowing and feeling that things would work out. I took a deep breath and went to find out what my options were.

Numerous flights had been canceled to New York because of an ice storm. I decided the resulting madness, frustration, and anger that hung in the air at the airport was something I didn't want to be a part of. Instead, I listened to my inner voice and chose to be who I wanted to be in the situation, which meant accepting that I might miss the event in New York and finding a way to be okay with it. I was just starting to get used to hearing and acting on those inner callings after so many years of ignoring them. I was beginning to trust that no matter how things turned out, there was always something larger at work than just my picture of how I wanted it to be. It also meant I needed to be calm and patient and start seeing the best in everyone around me.

I waited in line at the gate of the US Airways counter for my now-canceled flight. In front of me was a woman whose flight had also been canceled. She was leaning over the counter and shaking her arms at the woman behind the desk. For every solution the attendant gave the woman, she'd roll her eyes and slam her hand down. Eventually, she stormed off. I felt so bad for the agent. She wasn't the one who had caused the bad weather. After listening to the woman in front of me do her best to make the agent feel awful, I made an extra effort to be nice to her when it came my turn.

"Thank you for waiting on me, and I promise I won't scream at you," I said to the agent.

She smiled, inhaled, and said, "Thank you."

I explained my dilemma. For several minutes, she did her best to find me another flight, but every available flight was leaving Pittsburgh after my event in New York was set to start.

We looked at each other in disappointment, and I slowly felt myself letting go and giving in to the thought, *Well, I guess I just won't make it, and there must be a good reason for it.*

Suddenly, the agent said, "I know!" She yelled across the terminal and asked another US Airways agent, "Did that flight leave yet?"

At the sound of a "No!" booming over the chitter chatter of waiting passengers, she quickly printed out a ticket for me and told me I was going to Ithaca. I called my event coordinator, who made arrangements for a driver to pick me up there, about sixty miles from my event.

I walked over to the new gate to find it completely deserted. I waited there for almost thirty minutes, growing steadily more concerned I was in the wrong place. What the hell was going on?

Eventually, another agent came up to me and asked, "Are you ready to go?"

Confused, I said, "To Ithaca, right?"

He nodded his head and asked me to follow him outside. He took out his umbrella, protected me from the rain, and walked me to the plane about twenty yards away. "You know you are the only one on this flight, right?"

It didn't quite sink in what he meant. I just followed along like I had been doing the last hour.

I walked up the stairs to get into the plane and peered around the corner. The stewardess was there to greet me, and behind her, every seat was empty. She opened her body up toward the aisle and gracefully pointed to the cabin while telling me to choose whichever seat I wanted.

I called Clare before we were all settled in to take off to tell her what had happened. She was in disbelief. Once I was buckled up, the pilot spoke over the loudspeaker, "Welcome, Meagan, we are taking you to Ithaca. Sit back and enjoy the ride."

A grin grew across my face as I nestled deeper into my seat. I couldn't believe my luck. I guess there was a break in the clouds or something, kind of like the parting of the Red Sea.

I made it in plenty of time for my event that night. I will always be thankful to US Airways for the valuable lesson I learned that day: the world will shift for you when fate needs to find a way. Often, situations don't unfold how we want them to, but I've learned to trust that no matter the outcome, my heart's deepest desires are held by the hands of God. There has always been a part of me that believes if I want something, things will find a way to work out. It's just that sometimes I want something else more than the thing I need. Maybe that's what writing this book was about: finding out where that belief was challenged and transformed into a new way of seeing how we are still held even when it doesn't feel like it.

While I was getting a lot of positive movement with my book, paying my way for everything was starting to wear on me. I traveled across the country for different promotional events, and while the sales were decent and my book was beginning to get published in other languages, it wasn't enough to make a living. I quit my boring job to free up my energy and gave self-employment a shot. Once again, I flabbergasted my family. My older brother sent me gas money when he heard the news.

I was making my way through a life coaching program and decided to start taking on paying clients. Clare was in my corner, encouraging me to get out and network. As an introvert, meeting new people has always been overwhelming for me, but Clare would take me to events and introduce me to everyone she knew. She didn't have much money either, so we held tightly to each other and made our way down a scary road of wondering how we were going to pay our bills. We moved into a basement apartment at a friend's house. I didn't tell my family about it for a long time. I was moving in with a woman they barely knew after only a year since my last breakup, and I was still embarrassed by our age difference.

Once I finished *It Is What It Is* and submitted it to my publisher, he turned it down because *Creating Your Heaven on Earth* wasn't making enough money for him to justify publishing another book of mine. That's when I started to question if I was heading down the right path. The lesson I had learned about following my heart in Ithaca was a powerful one, but through my struggles, it was easy to forget. I was being guided, but I didn't know where I was being guided to. I had never questioned my writing before then. I did try submitting the same book to other places, but nothing ever came of it. I needed to pay my bills, but the athlete in me also demanded results, and because I couldn't see them, I started to feel like a failure. I wanted to feel like a success. I wanted to feel important.

I decided to focus my energy on building my coaching business. Between my clients and Clare's two jobs, we were able to afford my travel. Life coaching was fun, but it wasn't writing. Nothing will ever replace writing, but I thought if I added more things to my repertoire, something would eventually fall into place. But I needed it to happen sooner rather than later. I was in a hurry to feel validated and show my family I was doing a good job with my life.

I continued to promote my book and create workshops and speaking engagements for myself to bring in extra income. I even made it on stage with Don Miguel Ruiz for an event in Syracuse, New York. Being on stage next to one of my favorite authors was a dream.

Before going on stage, I was pacing back and forth, trying to keep the nausea from turning into anything more. Don Miguel noticed my discomfort, walked over to me, and placed his hands on my shoulders. "Everyone is going to hear you. Be careful what you say."

I shook my head like a child obeying their father. I took his words to mean, "Because of who you are, people are going to listen, so choose your words wisely." The pressure was on to perform.

I hadn't planned what I was going to say. I'd decided to leave it to Spirit. My lack of preparation led me to let go and trust my inner voice, the Spirit within me. If my talk wasn't recorded, I wouldn't have remembered any of it. The message was about living your heaven on Earth by trusting God to lead you. I told the audience, "If you have a vision, a dream, a passion, then hold onto that. Everything that is meant to go hand in hand with what is inside your heart is happening already."

That's what I thought I was doing at the time, but after the event, I kept moving further and further away from the rawness of my work and diving more into what I thought was going to make me look good enough to become successful.

I stopped writing as much and started searching for content that would sell. Instead of just writing from my heart and being myself, like I did with my book that got published, I started writing to fit what I thought the world wanted to hear. I began to look for validation in everything I did, and an emptiness started to form.

At one point, I was asked to cohost a live radio interview with a famous psychic. During the show, she wanted to give my co-host and me a reading. She peered through my eyes and into my soul, pointed her finger at me, and said, "You don't know what you are doing or where you are going."

I was completely perplexed. Of course I knew where I was going! Looking back, it's clear that I was way off course. I was saying yes to every new shiny object, and it was leaving me dull.

Life became heavy as I searched for a feeling of worthiness, but that feeling wouldn't come through work. It had to come from me. I was trying to find self-acceptance by making myself palatable to others while also trying to find genuine connection by being my most honest and authentic self. It wasn't an easy path to navigate. In fact, for a long time, the path didn't feel like a path at all. I thought I knew so much, but I would soon realize that, if anything, I knew very little.

Owning who we are is hard work. But it is worth it.

PART II

SHARE

Sharing isn't about just talking. It's about being willing to let others see you in your fullness.

CHAPTER 10

Standing in front of my friend's kitchen window, the foothills of Colorado pulled me into a trance as I let the water at the sink run hot. The snowcapped mountains seemed to morph into towering magnolia trees just starting to bloom. I was being called back to Mississippi. I kept my hands under the water despite the stinging heat and furiously scrubbed the dishes, attempting to keep my nausea at bay. It didn't work. After being gone for so long, was I really being guided to go back? I was terrified. I couldn't brush it off. The calling was clear.

The Universe was laying out a path for me. The end of the path was vibrant, even though the way was unclear. Something bigger than me knew it was time to fully step into my own healing. I had to go back to Mississippi if I truly wanted to love myself because I could only find the type of acceptance I was looking for if I could learn to be my authentic self at home, despite the deep hurt the place had caused me.

My older brother had his son, my first nephew, which made the pull toward Mississippi even stronger. The writing was on the wall, but I didn't want to see it. Clare, a trained acupuncturist, was doing medical transcription nights and weekends and was managing office spaces that were rented by corporations during the day. We were both working hard to earn a living, but neither of us was so grounded in our work that we couldn't start over somewhere new.

We had been going back and forth between Colorado and Mississippi quite a bit. During one of those visits, we were rocking on a swing on my parents' back porch. Clare and I were talking about moving to Mississippi when she told me about a memory she had from her childhood.

"I used to dream of living in Mississippi. I envisioned myself sitting on a front porch next to a Magnolia tree."

I started rocking faster to keep up with the pace of my heart.

Clare had never been to the South before she met me. I argued, "I just don't think I can do it. I can't move back here." A part of me wanted to, but the other part of me was just too scared.

She looked at me, put her foot down on the ground to stop the rocking, and with clarity said, "Let's move here."

I knew she was right. I had a job opportunity to take care of a friend's ninety-three-year-old father, which was a start. I was becoming stagnant in Colorado professionally, and I really wanted to watch my nephew grow up and see how my work would develop as I focused on loving myself in Mississippi.

I was petrified because Mississippi brought up all of my insecurities, shame, and self-deprecation. My self-doubt was taunting me in Colorado, but I knew Mississippi would amplify my fears and either force me to deal with them or push me to the edge. Either I was going to learn to love myself or push everything good out of my life because I didn't believe I deserved any of it.

Clare went back to Colorado to pack our things, and I was left behind to start working to find us a place to live. When the owner of the first house I viewed became aware I would be living with another woman, she made up some lame excuse as to why she couldn't rent to us. In fact, when I found the house we ended up living in, I lied to the landlord and said that I would be living alone. He lived in Georgia, so there was no reason he would ever find out.

I was fresh from Colorado, and I had already started lying again. I didn't know who I could trust, so honesty was reserved for those I felt safe with. Lying about who I was made me uncomfortable in my own skin. My heart took a hit each time it happened.

I knew I was going to run into people who had hurt me and people who I thought would hurt me at the grocery store, at the post office, or at restaurants. I was especially terrified of running into people who'd scarred me before, like Darius from the chapel. If I saw him, what would I say or do? I'd probably hide or act like I didn't see him. Facing him would mean facing myself.

I wasn't ready to answer questions like, "So, are you married?" "Do you have a boyfriend?" or "Do you have kids yet?"

When I went back to Colorado to help Clare finish packing and tie up loose ends, it was time to say goodbye to our beloved friends. The community we created around us was supportive and loving, and I was devastated to leave them. To find a community that loved me for all of me was fulfilling, but not fulfilling enough to keep me in Colorado. I wanted to love myself, and I couldn't accomplish that if I stayed put. As we were getting ready to leave, crying and hugging our way through our goodbyes, we were talking about how we didn't have any money left after paying for the U-Haul. Our dear friend dug into her purse and pulled out a one-hundred-dollar bill. That is the money that got us to Mississippi.

If I didn't have Clare, I am not sure I would have ever moved back to Mississippi. She was the strength I couldn't gather within myself. She still is. When I think about that time in my life now, I think about how grateful I am for her. She took a risk . . . for me. She has the same sense of adventure and following her heart without knowing what's next that I do. That's why we work. We move through the world willing to change directions when our hearts lead us elsewhere. She's the kind of life partner I was looking for, but she is more than that. She's the other half of me. When I'm down, she lifts me up, and when she is down, I lift her up.

When our journey in Mississippi began, we knew we would have our challenges, but we didn't know how hard it would be to be openly gay. At least I didn't have to do it alone.

In August of 2010, Clare and I moved into our first house in Mississippi. The adjustment to being back home required emotional preparation I didn't realize I would need. Any confidence I'd built up over the years while I was gone went flying out of the window once I realized how hard it was to be honest about being a gay woman and a non-Christian spiritual thinker.

Clare and I lived in a cute little cottage that served as a safe haven for us in some ways—except when I needed to call the landlord for maintenance issues. My fear would outweigh my pride of living with Clare, and my sense of security would disappear.

"Go upstairs and keep quiet while I talk to him," I'd say to Clare whenever it was time for the landlord to come by. I knew if he found out I was living with another woman, he might ask us to leave.

She never fought me on it, as she understood what the ramifications would mean.

Whenever I called him, I could feel myself slipping into a fight or flight mindset. I was the victim, but I wanted control. Jumping back into the closet wasn't what I wanted to do when we moved back to Mississippi, but sometimes, my only focus was getting through the day in one piece.

My lack of self-acceptance was running my life. I felt like I was in jail whenever I was around town, and sometimes whenever I was in my own house. Either I was going to have to start putting myself out there more or fall into a tailspin of voices that tried to remind me *I was not good enough*. The darkness forming within needed some light, and I had to be the one to shine it.

One way I did that was by accepting odd jobs to meet new people.

A friend of ours offered for us both to work with her on a few projects. She worked for a local photographer, and they needed help when they went into the school district to take everyone's yearly photos. We said yes to every job we were offered because we got to work together. However, once our friend's boss figured out Clare and I were a couple, all hell broke loose. I don't remember how he found out, but we were asked not to come back to work.

Because I was substitute teaching at the time, the man's wife was able to access my files at the school district's administrative offices. She wanted to make sure I had passed my background check. I assume her rationale was that because I was gay, I was also a child molester or a criminal.

The owner of the business knocked on our door several days after we were fired. I ran upstairs because I couldn't muster the courage to face him. His behavior shrank me back to silence and isolation. The lump in my throat was telling me to speak up, but my anger scared me. In this case, anger was a sign that strength was forming and that I was beginning to draw some lines. I wasn't willing to accept what was happening, but was I willing to do something about it?

Clare made me come downstairs and face him. I walked down the stairs slowly, and as I reached the bottom, I looked to the right. There he was. Just the sight of him made my stomach turn in knots.

I sat down across the room from him. I could hear him whimpering, so my eyes made their way toward his old dirty shoes, to his pants with too many pockets, to his button-down short-sleeve shirt, and up to his pale white cheeks that were covered in tears.

"I am so embarrassed by my wife's actions and my own."

I turned away to hide my own tears. His words were giving my anger permission to let down the walls.

"I've never been around a gay couple before. I asked you to not come back to work because I was afraid the school district would fire me if I kept y'all on my staff."

I couldn't just sit there and keep listening.

"Your wife went into my files. She's assuming I am a criminal because I am gay. Do you have any idea how that makes me feel? It makes me feel like the scum of the earth. It hurts."

He put his hands in his face and leaned over in shame. "Please come back to work for me. I am so sorry."

I didn't hesitate. "No. I am willing to forgive you, but I will not work for you again."

As much as I appreciated his self-reflection and courage to come forward and apologize, the damage had been done, so I set us both free. I forgave him, and I stuck to my boundaries. He is still, to this day, one of the few who has expressed any remorse. He taught me I could be exposed and rejected and choose to forgive the offender while still standing my ground. For my own peace, I've had to learn to do the harder thing and choose to forgive those who haven't offered an apology at all. What's made that a bit easier is never expecting one in the first place.

Mississippi has a dark, deep-seated history of prejudice. If you aren't white, heterosexual, and Christian, then you are the "other." The current state of affairs often feels as heavy as the state's history. I felt it when we moved there in 1989, and the same feeling remained when we moved back in 2010. While parts of the Magnolia State appeared to have it together, there was an underlying stagnancy. I could relate. I felt stuck when others saw strength and confidence. The world around me was showing me myself, and it was going to be quite the undertaking to transform my insecurities into wholeness.

Clare and I were constantly talking about the life we wanted for ourselves, and while we weren't where we wanted to be financially, we knew we were capable of figuring it out. Taking care of a ninety-three-year-old man wasn't what I had in mind for my first job when we moved back to Starkville, but it paid the bills. I also began working with my parents, painting houses inside and out. Clare got a gig tutoring two little boys after school, and she also began teaching English as a second language to a couple from Korea. We felt like we'd hit it big whenever we could afford to buy a six pack of Bud Light and rent a Redbox movie.

I was still promoting my book, but the energy I was putting into surviving and getting used to being back in Mississippi was eating up my inspiration. We created vision boards and talked every morning about our dreams. At that point, we both believed there was a way to co-create our dream lives with God, and we were determined to figure it out. In retrospect, I can see self-acceptance has been the consistent answer to all of our doubts, insecurities, and unknowns. That self-acceptance gave us the confidence to support each other in our personal journeys to love ourselves.

As the internal self-work continued, I realized it was time to have some hard conversations I'd been avoiding over the years with family members. If I wanted a deep connection with my family, I couldn't ignore it anymore. I had to clear things up.

CHAPTER 11

My mom struggled when we first moved back. She was distant, often sitting in silence when we were in the same room. I wondered if I was the reason for her distance and felt forced to face my role of feeling responsible for her happiness.

After we had only been in Mississippi for a few weeks, Clare told me about a conversation she had with my mom when they went for a walk. Clare told me, "I asked her how she was doing with us being here."

"And what did she say?" I was anxious to stop guessing.

"Your mom seemed uncomfortable with my question, but she answered pretty quickly. She said, 'I just don't understand it. I don't get it.'" I didn't get it, either. How could she buy Desiree gifts during the holidays and welcome Clare to Mississippi and still be struggling with accepting who I was?

Shaking my head, I responded with exhaustion, "I just don't understand."

Clare put her hand on my leg, "I told her that she never will understand what it is like to be gay. She just has to accept it. A light bulb went off in her eyes. It was like she had never thought of that before."

I put my hand on top of Clare's and squeezed it with gratitude.

My mom was doing inner work to come to terms with my sexuality. My dad and I spent time talking about religion and spirituality. We were both searching for answers to our own personal dilemmas. He, after having lost his business of over twenty years and their house, was at rock bottom.

I could feel the defeat all over my dad, but he kept dreaming and trying and hoping. We would go for walks and have revealing conversations about who God was to us. I told him what I had learned over the years, and he listened. When I was struggling with my mom and my relationship, I could always call and talk to him about things. He was tough on me as a kid, which had its own effects on my self-esteem, but I knew I could trust his love for me, his acceptance of my being gay, and his respect for my partners. He was always the first to introduce Clare as my partner, then my wife, even before I could do it. He gave me courage.

He got back up and kept going to create a new life for my mom and himself. My mom got a job working at the National Fastpitch Coaching Association as an assistant to the director, and my dad began to dive into his new construction business.

My mom doesn't hide her feelings. I've always loved that about her. If you are sad, she will hug you and make you cry. Her love is tangible. She wanted to understand me, but understanding me was never going to be possible. She was wrestling with so much. Having lost their financial security and then having to face her gay daughter coming home must have felt overwhelming. Being the honest and open woman that she is, she had to deal with her insecurities because hiding isn't her mojo either. I know it wasn't easy.

It was time to clear the air with my mom after being in Mississippi for over a year. I asked her to write a letter to me about her perception and experience of my coming out day, and I would do the same. I was stuck reliving my coming out day and all of the pain that came with it. My pain specifically landed on her, and I desperately wanted to get past it. We both wrote raw and honest accounts of our experiences.

Agreeing to write those letters and following through took immense courage and an underlying vulnerability and trust in each other, but I realized I needed to go through this process with my mom to experience further healing, and she was on board without hesitation. We each wrote our letters without reading the other's, and when we were done, we shared our letters and then had a conversation about them. The letters read:

Dear Mom,
I remember the day—the day I told you I was gay. I had been with a woman for a year by then, and hiding it from you was so painful that I needed to get it out there . . . out of me. With uncertainty and a bit of courage within me, it seemed as though the road had paved itself as your house inched closer, one block of concrete at a time. I drove from my house to yours,

tears lodged in my throat . . . making their way to my eyes as my anxiety rose. I was so afraid, so afraid of what you would think. After disconnecting myself emotionally from you for a year, I was so distant from all that I knew, and I needed to find a way back home—back home to whoever I was missing behind my jumbled self-doubt. I was making a sincere leap and desperate attempt to find myself by coming to you, hoping you would have the answers.

When I arrived at your house on that hot, sunny Mississippi August day, you were outside in the garage. I think I remember you talking to someone who was leaving. As I got out of the car and walked toward you, you could tell something was wrong. You asked me, "What's wrong? Are you okay?" My tears were fighting for their life, but I think what had been buried for so long could not sit another moment inside of me, and so they began to stream down my face—my innocent face. I was so young and had just begun to open my eyes to the crueler side of people. You put your arms around me and led me to the living room. I could sense that you were unsure and confused about the reason for my tears. I was unsure too.

As we sat down on the couch, I finally uttered a few words: "I am not who you think I am. I am different than most girls." I remember when your confused expression turned into a fearful one once you realized what I was trying to say. I remember it like it happened yesterday. And maybe that's why I need to write this now . . . to move on, to let go of that moment. I have been holding this tightness in my chest, as we have never talked about this time—never consciously moved through it together. For the past several years, we have grown into a duo of trust again, a duo of connection. Our mother-daughter bond has grown to new heights . . . beyond understanding because we were never able to really understand; we had to leap higher than that. I pushed you, and you pushed me, and we got here together. But I want to move further still, and that will require that this day—"the day"—be forgotten as the worst day of my life and embraced as the best. I am ready to let go, and somewhere inside of me I know you are too. We are the same, the two of us. The same behind our fears, the same behind the need to be loved, the same behind it all. Behind it all, we are the same.

On that day, on the couch, when you began to cry, my world shattered. My heart broke as I realized I could never be who you wanted me to be. Or at least, that is how I took it. You said it before I could: "You mean, you are gay?" I nodded in dismay while behind your blank stare you processed the unwelcome information. You were my biggest mirror. I grew more and more silent, more and more distant as I realized you weren't going to be able to give me what I needed.

Self-acceptance has been a battle since that day for me. The deepest parts of me have been longing to let go of the rejection I have placed on myself over the years since then, from that one moment. And I feel that if I can heal this time in my life, then something will shift for me. To that you would say, "Do it for you, Meagan, not for me. Let go and just love who you are." I am trying, really. You have told me that over the last few years, and with every new change, I take another step, and each step has led me here—to openly acknowledging you let me down that day. I translated your fear into rejection. You didn't embrace me the way I had hoped; you embraced me, but your confusion reflected my own. And there we were, two people who loved each other tremendously, suddenly foreign to one another—like we abruptly jumped into a past life that vaguely made some sense, but not enough sense. You hugged me when I left, after Dad and the boys had come over to share in the big surprise, but it wasn't the same. I left with a weight lifted, but in its place, I wondered if we would ever make it back to the day before "the day."

We gritted our teeth as we tried to move forward. I know I put up a wall, and I am sorry for that. I am sorrier that I couldn't give you the daughter, the woman, you had hoped I would be. There is a sorrow I have kept stored over the last ten years, stored for right now. I noticed it was still lingering the other day when I couldn't enjoy a perfect moment—that there was still something inside that needed to come out. And when I closed my eyes this morning and asked The U (Universe) for some help, an image of "the day" popped into my mind immediately. I have long avoided this moment, today, as I have been afraid of feeling what I felt so long ago: that if I tell you that you let me down then we would be disconnected again. It is even harder to tell you that you let me down when I know you were just afraid in that moment, as I am sure you were reliving your own childhood memories of being bullied and made fun of, reliving your family breaking up, and not knowing what would be in store for me as an openly gay woman in Mississippi. I understand your fears now, but then, I didn't.

I know, Mom, that you cannot give me joy and fulfillment. That is not what I am asking for. In fact, I am not asking for anything. I know you love and accept all of me now and all the joy and fulfillment my life is blossoming into, and I know I see you now and all the joy and fulfillment you are blossoming into. I just can't hold onto "the day" anymore. I needed to revisit it, actually relive it from a space of knowing that it doesn't matter anymore. That day can no longer be what I remember. It doesn't fit who I see in front of me each time we visit . . . myself. I need and want to let you love all of me now.

And tonight, I look forward to our weekly dinner, with Clare and me, you, and dad. I look forward to it more now than ever as I sit here realizing that in the days before "the day," that's what we used to do—have dinner together every week. Here we are again.

I love you,

Meagan

Dear Meagan,

It's almost like a dream when I think back to the day you told me you were gay. So much has been lived since then.

"Mom!" your voice cracked as you said it over the phone. I knew something was not quite right when I heard my name. My heart fell some, and I thought, Please, not right now, Megs. Remember, I was in Jackson, Tennessee, with my dear friend Ann who was battling lung cancer? Ann didn't know me that day, which made it even harder to be there with her. I had been making those six-hour trips one day a week for some time, now knowing I would not be having many more.

"I need to see you as soon as you get home!" You were so insistent. I tried to put you off but couldn't. On the ride home, I could not think of anything that could be that urgent. I even called you back to try to get you to tell me over the phone, but you would not have it. Needless to say, the drive home was long, and my heart was already heavy from being with Ann.

You met me at the house. You were so nervous. I felt bad for you, but in my mind I was thinking, It's not as bad as she thinks. It can't be.

You sat down beside me on the couch, and before you could get it out, "You don't really know me," you started to sob. My *heart broke for you. I took you in my arms, and then you told me. I cannot remember the exact words in how you told me you were gay. I kind of shut down. I went numb. My ears started to ring. I could only think, I need your dad here with us. He has always been my rock, and I needed him there to hold me up so I could gain strength from him to hold you up. I realized in that moment our lives would never be the same. Change was evident. I know that I told you I loved you because that was what I was feeling, but the questions that were storming through my mind were deafening. I was so confused . . . you had dates, boyfriends . . . My mind was reeling. I was shaking with disbelief.*

When I looked at you and saw your pain, my heart broke for you. I then felt fear for you. What will everyone think? What will they say or do to you? Fear set in, and it stayed heavy in my heart for a very long time. I had to protect you! No one was to know!

I remember calling your brothers and dad and pleading with them to come home. I needed all of us to be together. I needed my family. You needed your family! I felt an urgency for us to be one and tell each other no matter what happened next that we love each other and will not turn our backs on each other. I needed to hear that as badly as you did. I went through that with my family with divorce, as you know, and I knew I could not bear it again.

That day was the beginning of a new life for all of us. As hard as it has been, it has also been very rewarding and rich with love and understanding. I know that I am a better person and mom for it. I truly live in the moment and cherish each opportunity that I can spend with my family—a true blessing. God has enriched our lives beyond measure, and I am grateful that my heart is no longer heavy with fear but with an amazing peace.

It took me a while, but I finally realized all I want to do is live in the truth and to love . . . let it be the way it is. God can take care of the rest!

I love you, my dearest daughter. You inspire me to embrace courage and be me,

Mom

I had no idea my mom had been in so much fear at the time. I knew she had a little fear, but I had thought that mostly she was just disappointed in me. And she had no idea I had felt rejected because of her fear. Her fear had been for me, not her. Together, we were able to put all the pieces together. All the time, I had been carrying the day I came out as a day of complete and utter rejection, when in reality, all she had wanted to do was love and protect me through it but didn't know how. She wasn't shown how by her own parents when her family split up, so she had to start from scratch. By communicating with honesty and openness, I was able to leap over a huge wall that had been standing in my way all those years.

It didn't take long for her to start encouraging me to love myself, but it took more conversations between us and the realization that my mom was grieving the life she thought I would have. At the time, marriage seemed unrealistic and having babies complicated. It just wasn't her picture for my life, and adjusting took some unwinding, time, and letting go.

It's not about being gay. I don't think it matters what the issue is. Every parent and child go through similar things. Parents tend to fear for their children (because the instinct is to protect), and children tend to feel rejected very easily by their parents. In my case, I found that my mom was mirroring my own insecurities. She never rejected me at all. She was just afraid for me. But I would have carried that load of rejection until the day I died unless I had said something.

As my mom and I were closing our conversation about our letters, she said with such conviction, "I love you. I love you. I love you, Meagan. I don't know how else to let you know that I love you . . . as you are."

This time, I let it in.

CHAPTER 12

As I was sitting on a bench outside of a local news station in 2013, sweat rolled down my back from the humidity. My palms and armpits were soaked with fear. The camera person was angling their lens to make it appear that Clare and I were holding hands.

I felt exposed.

Clare and I were being questioned about our thoughts and feelings around Proposition 8 and the Defense of Marriage Act (DOMA).

The thought of being more vocal was incredibly scary for me, but this urge to be vulnerable about my experiences wouldn't go away, so I kept putting myself out there in an attempt to become more comfortable in my own skin. I needed lying and hiding about my life to be a thing of the past. I needed to be honest no matter the consequences.

It all started by writing a blog to share my story and experiences as a gay woman. I needed to do it for me. I needed to voice my fears and pain and find a way to work through my own issues around who I am. I was making progress in my relationships, but I wanted to be more vocal.

That's how this opportunity to be on the news arrived. The producers called me after reading my blog and wanted to interview me on my thoughts of the ruling. They even asked Clare to come along.

I had a mix of both joy and fear after the United States v. Windsor SCOTUS ruling. I'm sure for most gay Mississippians—like for me—their coming-out experience was traumatic on some level. Decisions like that one open old wounds and bring the conversation to the forefront. For any oppressed community or group of people—Black, Jewish, Hispanic, Muslim, gay, it doesn't matter—it's not easy to talk about the fears lurking behind closed doors. And while I was excited about the rulings, the feeling that the other shoe was about to drop lingered.

In Mississippi, our history of oppression and segregation still hangs thick in the air, but most people would rather avoid talking about it. However, in order to heal and move forward, we have no choice but to talk about it. At the time, I thought about those who opposed gay marriage. I saw them as being afraid their beliefs and ideas about marriage were being confronted with something different. Ironically, I was afraid too. I was afraid of being rejected as gay marriage became a bigger topic in Mississippi. But if you put fear and fear together, the result is tension, avoidance, anger, injustice, and the need to be right by pointing outward rather than inward. The same is true of any issue that separates us and causes us to discriminate against others. Fear is fear, and love is love. I didn't want to be afraid, so I was willing to risk my peace in order to work through it. I wasn't trying to change other people's minds. I was trying to change my view of myself.

When Clare and I arrived at the station, we were greeted with hugs and acceptance. One of the news anchors came specifically to hug me and compliment me on my blog. The person who interviewed Clare and me that morning told us that she had called numerous couples to interview along with us, and they had all declined. She said they were worried about their bosses finding out who they were and losing their jobs as a result. I understood. We were not protected by the law in Mississippi. We still aren't. As business owners, we had a lot at stake too. On the flip side, it was just as hard for the network to find a preacher who was willing to be interviewed about why they were not in support of gay marriage. It was clear to me then that we are all just afraid of being rejected or cast aside.

The interview gave me an opportunity to see how far I had come in embracing more of myself. I had stomach jitters before it aired, as you never know what clips they are going to show from the entirety of the time you spend talking on camera.

A reverend from a Baptist church in Starkville appeared in the clip first. He was not happy with the court's decision.

"I'm in disagreement with how they're defining marriage now through the Supreme Court. However, I'm not against people who have been together in same-sex unions getting the benefits that I believe they deserve. But from a biblical standpoint, I believe marriage is strictly between a man and a woman."

People throughout the state were mixed on the ruling. The news anchor went on to quote comments from different social media outlets. "It's a no-brainer. The majority can't deny the minority rights. It's, you know, unconstitutional. A bible is irrelevant to US law."

But someone else disagreed. "Sad day in America. Religious freedoms, definition of marriage, and our political system were torn apart today."

The reverend came back on the screen to say one more thing, "I think we will attract more people by loving them rather than condemning them."

Attract? Is he serious?

Suddenly I saw myself pop up on the screen. I hid my face, then opened my fingers one at a time to see through the cracks.

"I was very nervous to come here and talk about this, but I knew it was calling me to be more courageous and more loving than I've ever been before. Because of that clash, you cannot live in fear forever, and we have to rise above that fear and learn to love each other."

The scene faded out with Clare and me on that bench looking like we were holding hands. We were exposed to the fullest, and there was no turning back. I was afraid of the responses we would receive the next day.

Right after the interview, we heard from preachers and patients, friends and strangers, blog followers and passersby—the whole town was abuzz. They praised us for our bravery and shared their joy in grins, handshakes, and hollers.

We were shopping at the grocery store days after the interview when we ran into some people who had watched it.

In the produce section, a preacher friend asked, "So, what kind of response are y'all getting from your interview?"

"It has been all positive so far."

Smiling, he whooped, "Well, praise the Lord."

As we made our way to the bakery, we saw one of our heterosexual friends who thought the interview was an impressive feat of courage. "I feel like I can do anything after seeing y'all do that interview!" she yelped.

We kept making our way through the store, and as I was pulling some yogurt out of one of the refrigerators, someone I didn't know walked up to me and said, "I know I don't know you, but kudos for going on WCBI. I know how risky it was, although you were already out. I hope you and your partner experience only good things from it."

Lugging groceries to the car, Clare and I discussed the unexpected, overwhelming support. Suddenly, a random woman saw us from a distance and yelled across two rows of cars, "Hey, I saw y'all on TV the other night. I am so happy for y'all! Congratulations!"

She ran over to shake both of our hands. The encouragement lit me up from the inside out.

Taking action, despite how terrified I was, set me free in a new way. Speaking from love and sharing my own experience in a place I previously could only associate with rejection transformed me from the inside. Truthfully, I've seen over the years that when I'm willing to be vulnerable, I, in turn, give others permission to be vulnerable too. This is where connection happens. I've never exposed my truest, purest heart and received hatred in return.

For years after, voicing my experiences gave me an opportunity to heal in different layers. Healing didn't happen for me overnight. I still have days when negative voices linger, but they are not nearly as loud as they used to be. I know how to control them now instead of being at their mercy. Vulnerability gave me the confidence I'd been seeking, but it gave me so much more than that.

I am not your typical activist. I am a vulnerable storyteller. I put my heart and feelings on the line because I never want to walk away from an interaction feeling like I didn't give enough of myself. I want a chance—a chance to open someone's else's heart and have a real connection. I've learned the power of telling my own story over and over and over to many different people in many different ways is what has given me the opportunity to move forward—baby steps, always baby steps.

CHAPTER 13

I was in the fourth grade when another girl tried to choke me with a purse strap.

We were on our way to an after-school Girl Scouts meeting. I jumped into the back of one of the parent's station wagons, and before I knew it, I couldn't breathe. I tried to get my fingers under the strap to break myself free but couldn't. One of the parents noticed my struggle and rushed to open the car door by the girl who was choking me. I don't remember much about what happened after that. After the girl was removed from the car, the parent checked on me, and while I was physically fine, I was panicking inside. I wondered what I had done to set the other girl off. I later found out that I hadn't done anything. No one ever knew why she choked me that day.

I was scared of that girl going forward. We later competed against each other in city sports and eventually became teammates in junior high and high school. I felt like she never really liked me, or perhaps the feeling of safety around her disappeared forever when she tried to choke me. She had an edge to her that kept me at a distance. When we became teammates, I found that when I celebrated her, I wasn't so scared.

I carried that pattern forward into high school, college, and adulthood. Perhaps it was a pattern that began at birth, an ancestral precedent that was set for me to either overcome or embrace. Either way, it was natural for me to ease the people around me to avoid my own discomfort. Being shy, I had to do it in ways that weren't bold or too noticeable, so I'd write people handwritten notes to tell them how awesome they were.

Kindness became a go-to for me. My mom is kind—the genuine and real kind. My great-grandmother, whom I am named after, was one of the kindest people around according to everyone who knew her. Kindness has always been my initial response to those outside of my family when things were tough, when tension arose, or when I was wronged in some way. I've always questioned whether that part of me has needed to please people or if I really am just nice. It's a battle I still roll around in my heart. Am I kind to make others comfortable and make myself appear likable, or am I kind because that is who I am? There is a difference. When I moved back to Mississippi, this internal battle continued to blossom in new ways. I still wanted to treat others right but not at the expense of communicating the truth about who I was. My truth was more important than other people's discomfort. The more I owned my reality, the more opportunities I had to do so.

Clare and I moved our businesses to a bigger location in 2013 because we were growing at an astounding rate. After we moved in, I had an experience with Darius, my spiritual mentor from the chapel, the one who told me I was going to hell, the same guy I had lied to about the real me.

What the hell do you do when your biggest fear walks through your door, slowly opening your deepest wounds simply with their presence?

There was no walking out, no turning around. I had butterflies—not the good kind. He was the mascot for the day all of Starkville found out I was gay. He wasn't the only one who told me I was going to hell, but he and his wife were etched in my mind as the characters who stole the show.

Transformation has a way of catching you in a moment of inadequacy and then gracefully reminding you your best self is ready to emerge. Along my path in Mississippi, I learned to trust in something deeper than my initial reactions, even if I couldn't see all the reasons why. The unknown became a friend I was learning to lean on. All the small steps had led me to this moment. This was one mountain I knew I could climb and survive. If I didn't fight, my path to wholeness was at risk.

As Darius leaned over the front counter to say something, I took a step back before leaning in to listen.

"Hey, I want to talk to you for a minute," he kind of said, kind of asked, as his booming voice took over the room and momentarily made me feel small. The trauma from the chapel lingered. *Didn't he ask me a similar question all those years ago when he wanted to talk to me?* Back then, I told him I didn't want to talk, but I caved because I thought I was ready to stand up for myself. In the end, I lied about who I was. This time, if I was put into a position to lie, I couldn't risk going back again. I couldn't climb my way out of that kind of self-defeat again.

I gripped the counter to steady myself and replied, "Sure, give me a second."

I ran off to the bathroom. Once the door was closed, I began to panic. I paced from the toilet to the door and to the mirror to look into my own eyes. *Can I do this?* Tears emerged. I splashed water on my face and watched my hands shake as I reached for a paper towel. Just as I thought I was going to break down, a voice within me said, *Who do you want to be right now?*

I was then able to see my fears for what they were. I was afraid of being rejected. More than that, I was afraid of not being authentic. I wanted to take off my mask in the face of anyone who terrified me. Right then, no one scared me more than Darius except myself. I needed to prove that I could handle any outcome, no matter what direction our conversation was about to take.

If I left my mask on, I'd suffer. If I took it off, he might have been uncomfortable. Maybe he was about to tell me I was going to hell—again. He had the power to push my spirit back into the flames of his righteousness where I'd, once again, lose myself.

I took a deep breath, calmed down, wiped my tears, and remembered the person I was beyond my label. I gripped the door handle to leave the bathroom and thought to myself, *I've got this.*

I walked back up front and around the counter. He reached out his hand to shake mine, and a surge of energy rushed through my body. I refused. My inner self, the one who knows better than my frightened self, took over the interaction before I had a chance to think. I opened my arms and went in for a hug. I was doing it again—curbing my fear by showing love to someone who made me feel scared. I don't know if he felt loved right then, but I felt love for him. It immediately became clear to me that being who you are and speaking from your heart doesn't always require words.

Our interaction showed me that no matter where my kindness comes from—whether it be real or manufactured to avoid discomfort—it shifts things for me. It allows me to open my heart and let go of my fears. While it isn't always easy, it's one of the few tools I've used consistently to pad myself from the feeling of rejection.

Darius had heard me on the news, but he didn't want to chat about me. He wanted to talk about the difference between life coaching and counseling and whether or not he should get his life coaching certificate. My fear lingered as I hung on to his every word, waiting for something. I didn't need him to apologize. I didn't need him to tell me that he hurt me. I just needed to be me. Would it have been helpful for me to tell him how his rant from years before affected me? Perhaps, but probably only for me. But he didn't, and I can't turn back time to see if speaking those words would have eased the years before or the years to come.

His business happened to be a block away from our new holistic center, so he had made the effort to walk over and chat. Maybe he was scared before he came to talk to me. Maybe he had to pray for half an hour beforehand. Maybe he had to get in touch with who he really was too.

People ask me all the time, "Why do you live in Mississippi?" They wonder why I would want my past and my wounds to be thrown in my face every day. Many people have said to me over the years, "Meagan, you don't have to walk in everyone's shoes. You don't always have to be kind. Remember, you are the one who has been wronged here." For a moment, when I hear people say this, I consider it. I think, *Yeah, it would be easier to close off my heart and put my fists up.* But then I remember that closing off my heart and fighting back isn't who I am. As much as I question myself, I lean on the part of me that wants to move forward with openness, even if it means sacrificing being the advocate that people want me to be.

It's taken a long time to embrace this part of myself. I still battle with it. Why can't I just tell someone I am scared of them? Why can't I just say, "What you did to me wasn't okay. It hurt." Why do I feel so compelled to break a barrier with kindness?

Being honest about my feelings—letting someone know they'd hurt me—didn't become a thing for me until many years after realizing that if I want to be my truest self, honesty is the only choice. Suffering became unbearable. Softness is still important to me, but it has to go hand in hand with sincere feelings. Otherwise, there is only half an opportunity to transform.

CHAPTER 14

When I walked into the TV station, I looked to my left, and there sat a man with a booming voice and bright white teeth encased in the curves of his lips as he smiled at me. I froze in a moment of uncertainty. I knew him. He was a Baptist pastor. We were friends, but he didn't know I was gay.

Years before, he had been the principal of a middle school where I was working pro bono as a life coach with his students. We worked together to help the kids, work that allowed us to see the truest parts of each other. I had been in working relationships before where I thought the other person saw me, only for them to reject me after finding out I was gay.

I checked in at the front desk and inched closer to my friend. My feet were heavy with anticipation. As his warmth grew cold, my lack of self-worth changed my perception of him. I reached out to shake his hand. *Wait, don't shake his hand.* He seemed reserved. Or was I just scared? I took a step closer and reached out for a hug. He leaned in to receive it. *I am okay. Everything is okay.*

My fear reappeared as I stepped away to go sit down. Now that I knew we would be interviewed together, the stakes seemed higher. This wouldn't be just any other pastor rejecting me. This time, it would be on air, from someone I knew. My legs were bouncing up and down as I sat and waited for the producer to call us back to the studio.

The producer greeted us in the lobby and said they were ready for us. I stood up and noticed my hands shaking, so I shoved them into my pockets and approached to shake her hand first. I put my hands back into my pockets as quickly as possible.

The station had called me that morning and asked if I would be willing to come in and talk about my perspective on same-sex commitment ceremonies in state buildings. This conversation was a hot topic at the time because a same-sex couple had applied to have a commitment ceremony in a state building in Jackson, Mississippi. This hadn't gone over well with most people, and there was no law in place to keep the couple's application from being dismissed. Ultimately, they were granted permission to have their ceremony, but most of the state was in an uproar. I was supposed to talk about how this made me feel as an openly gay woman.

Even though my previous interview with Clare had gotten a good reaction, this one elicited different fears for me. Having a mediated debate was risky. I could be rejected on TV.

I had learned by then that if I wanted to overcome my fears, I had to be willing to act when I felt them, so I said yes to the interview. My heart was pounding when I got off the phone. I was more nervous than I had ever been. Threats I'd received since returning to Mississippi swarmed in my head: "Get off the streets, lesbians!" "Go back where you came from!" "You are going to burn in hell."

I felt like throwing up. My angst was so deep that I was afraid I would walk out of that television station and someone would shoot me. The first openly gay mayor in Mississippi was murdered, and an openly gay male friend of mine was beaten to death a few years after I left Mississippi. To be openly gay seemed like a death sentence.

But the bigger part of me knew I could do it and that I could do it well. Clare encouraged me, gently prodding, "You were made for moments like this." I had been consciously working on my self-confidence and had realized I felt called to speak out as an openly gay person in Mississippi in a loving way that honored my true nature. So, after years of developing my self-acceptance, I knew this interview was an opportunity to express myself in a way that was from my heart.

I focused on the bigger picture. As much as there is a part of me that wants to fight those who can't seem to see past my sexuality, and as much as I want to push those away who want to openly reject me, there is still a part of me that knows I would never be satisfied with that. That part of me is in everyone, the part of our human essence that sees everyone for who they are: different, unique, and equal. I knew I was ready, even though my fear of rejection on television was both real and validated by my past.

As we sat down on the set, we shared very little conversation. We avoided each other's eyes while facing the cameras that were going to project a fraction of who we were. I kept shifting in my seat while he repeatedly cleared his throat. There we sat, waiting for the cameras to roll: him, a pastor of a Southern Baptist church; the host, a congregate at his church; and me, the gay girl.

The host told me not to be nervous as she glanced down at my tightly clasped hands. "It isn't the cameras that make me nervous," I confessed.

I had been interviewed a million times before, but not like this. The producer assured me this was to be an equal conversation and she didn't want anyone to feel like they were backed in a corner. In my mind, it was two against one already, so I had to close my eyes and access the part of me that was saying, *Just be yourself and speak your truth. You are them, and they are you.*

A space opened for truth to enter. I saw clearly that I was beautiful as I was and could say what I needed to say without feeling like I needed to protect myself, hide myself, or feel like a victim to the situation. Getting there took closing my eyes, accessing my heart, and choosing to only take responsibility for my own words and actions, the only true empowerment.

After I opened my eyes, the interview began.

The host started with me. "Does the ruling really matter that much to you?"

My voice was shaking. "As a person who is gay, it's important that I feel like I can be who I want to be and choose where

I want to go if I want to have an event of my own. So, to me, it makes me feel more like an equal instead of a person who is less than everyone else."

How did I sound? Did I say the right thing?

The attention shifted to the pastor. "I imagine that this conversation for you is one that's difficult to have with your congregation. Tell us your reaction first to this opinion about the law," the host said.

The preacher stumbled on his words and answered, "I think it's just that it's the law, and the law explicitly says what it desires, and we have to deal with that accordingly because as United States citizens, we're governed by those laws. What has happened is, a people issue has become a political issue, and it is now polarizing our country. When we make people issues political issues, then people get lost in the mix, and we have to be able to sit down and have honest and open conversations and be able to agree to disagree."

What did he just say?

The host jumped back in. "It's a people issue, it's a political issue, and it's also a religious issue—one that you know churches are having a conversation about now. They're having to address this with spiritual people and what they believe about gay relationships."

The preacher interjected, "Being a Baptist pastor, there are certain things that we believe hold true. I think what happens is, as Christians, we write sins or we rank the symptoms of sins that we consider to be wrong, but I am of the belief that anything that's outside of the will of God is right there together, and we don't have a right to say that this is a greater or lesser than."

I was looking at him, and he was looking past me straight at the host. I was wedged between the two.

"So what I try to teach my congregation is that when you have a personal relationship with God, he lets you know according to his word and his will those things that each of us have to work on in our lives to try to better ourselves to line up with this direction."

Feeling smaller and still empowered to check in with my own beliefs, I wondered, *How can he possibly know what everyone's relationship with God is like?*

"Meagan, I don't know what your religious beliefs are, but how do you react to the religious community that's so vehemently against gay lifestyles and gay marriage in the state of Mississippi?" the host asked.

Sadness rolled in on a deep sigh. "I'll be honest with you, it's challenging. But at the end of the day, for me it's important to look at myself and ask myself if I was a good person."

I kept my eyes on the host, my only source of comfort on that stage.

"So when I am challenged with something that might make me angry or make me feel hurt or make me question myself, it's important that when I lie down to go to sleep at night that I ask myself, *Was I loving today? Was I compassionate today? Was I honest today? Was I all of the things today that I want to be in the world?* It's about me taking personal responsibility for my life and my relationship with God and making sure I am in alignment with whatever I believe. It's really about me just being okay with who I am."

Phew. I don't know where that came from, but yes, it is a personal journey for everyone.

"Pastor, is it possible to disagree with the way someone lives or what they believe and still lovingly try to convey to them what you think is right?" asked the host.

He sat up taller. "I do believe that's possible, and that's the tricky part because when it comes to religious matters, we become dogmatic, and being dogmatic never really persuades people over to the side you're trying to get them on." He continued, "I know Meagan. We've worked together, and she did a wonderful job in a lot of areas. Even saying that, I still have beliefs about homosexuality that I would like to share with her."

Please don't share your opinions with me.

"In fact, she just heard my opinion, but that won't stop me from hugging Meagan or loving Meagan because that is what we're called to do as Christians."

The host chimed in, "Because Meagan is a good person, and I think we can all tell that from what we've learned today."

Shaking on the inside, I thought, *So I have to be a good person to be loved and accepted for who I am?* Something felt off, but the lights faded, and the interview was over.

Fear can cause you to either run away or access your core. In the interview, I dove into the deep, uncomfortable, scary place that we often avoid, and I found myself. I didn't blame anyone for anything. I wasn't angry. I simply showed up. That one act pushed me into a new dimension of approval of myself beyond right and wrong. It was a turning point I didn't shy away from, and it proved to me that while my beauty may be different, it's not inferior to anyone else's.

After the interview, I cried tears of relief—relief that I had made it through, relief that I hadn't felt rejected, relief that I had realized I could choose to be a victim or not in any situation.

As long as I feel I am a victim in any situation, I will most likely choose to fight back, and that accomplishes nothing for me and brings any conversation to a halt. That interview taught me that if I wanted to accept myself, I needed to make choices that were in alignment with who I really am and who I want to be.

CHAPTER 15

Mississippi State invited me to be the keynote speaker for their first annual National Coming Out Day event.

When I got the email, I ran to Clare's office to share the news, and she grabbed me in her excitement. As she was squeezing her hope into me, she whispered, "You've got this."

While it was exhilarating news, the fear of rejection loomed from my past. This was the first time I would be going back to campus to share my story, and it was going to be in the same building where I had received that phone call from Darius years ago.

It was 2013, several months after the interview with the Baptist pastor. At the time, the climate for LGBTQ+ people in Mississippi was slowly changing, but it still had a long way to go. It's not that people aren't accepting in Mississippi; they just don't get called to task often. They don't want to deal with their own discomfort around the differences of others in fear their views of God and the world will be at risk. I have often thought religious views give us a container to hold our thoughts and beliefs in, and breaking it means we no longer have a sense of control. As a result, controversial issues get swept under the rug with all our other Southern dirty laundry where they remain until someone ruffles some feathers. It's not that I wanted to ruffle feathers, but I did want to share my heart. The feathers just came with it.

Leading up to my keynote speech experience at Mississippi State, I knew I needed to prepare myself and go deep within. I spent much of that time quietly working on my new book, *Courage: Agreeing to Disagree Is Not Enough*. I wrote that book to try to etch doubt and fear out of my life. Moving through my own emotions and feelings of the cultural climate, my relationships, and my emotional and mental state was no easy task. While there were many LGBTQ+ people living in Mississippi, at the time, we didn't have any rights under the law. Patience demanded I face many of my own fears of rejection by standing on stage where I had been rejected before.

I titled my talk for my speech after my unpublished book. I chose this topic because when I came out of the closet, what people said most was, "I love you, Meagan, but I don't agree with being gay." From the moment I came out until the moment I stepped on the stage for my Homecoming Project on National Coming Out Day (of all days), I had been working on loving myself and finding a way to love those who opposed me so I wouldn't be someone who would say, "I love you, Bob, but I don't agree with the way you think being gay is wrong." I didn't want to be what others had been to me. I wanted to feel empowered by not putting other people down. The only way I knew how was to be by myself and not focus on what others thought and believed about me.

A few weeks before the event, I was extremely nervous and unsure of the response I might receive, but I had built up faith in my community. That year, major events in my life were spread out in a way that allowed me to grow and process accordingly. The talk at Mississippi State was well attended and one of the proudest moments of my life.

Just before I went on stage, I noticed people from the Starkville community layering into the rows, including my parents and some of their friends. I rummaged through the unfinished pages of my book, trying to find the parts that I wanted to share. I paced backstage as I watched reporters and their cameras file into the auditorium. My LGBTQ+ friends rolled in with excitement for an event meant just for them.

After I was introduced, I walked up the stairs and faced the audience. Everything in me wanted to walk back down the stairs and leave, but I didn't. I shared my story and my thoughts and feelings about how to deal with controversy. I wasn't sure how anyone—straight or gay, religious or not—would feel about my unapologetic stance.

I began by reading an excerpt from my book, *Courage: Agreeing to Disagree Isn't Enough*:

Agreeing to disagree is not enough. It sends a message that one is better than the other—or at least that's how I feel when I hear it. I believe we have to do better for our fellow people than agreeing to disagree by encouraging them to be who they are, to be who they want to be, to be who they feel called to be, and to follow their heart on their journey. If we do that, then equality will happen naturally.

I then dove into my story and the many lessons I had learned on my journey. I talked about my coming out story and how deeply hurt I was by the Fellowship of Christian Athletes. In telling my story, I recounted how the Fellowship of Christian Athletes had been the one organization to discriminate against me the most. I didn't focus on blaming or pointing the finger, I just simply stated what had happened, how it had felt, and how I had grown as a person because of it.

When I was done with my speech, I got a standing ovation. People celebrated me. It wasn't what I expected. Tears started streaming down my face as my parents made their way through the crowd to embrace me. No one wanted to leave that auditorium that night, so we all decided to go out to eat to celebrate Mississippi State's very first National Coming Out Day.

Our arrival at the restaurant was surreal. We took up an entire room of tables. My parents were sitting in the corner with their friends, who had a gay son. I glanced around at all of my LGBTQ+ friends smiling and laughing. I slipped into the moment of freedom and appreciated who I was and everyone there.

The following day, the local news put my story on the front page of the paper, and then the same article ran in Mississippi State's campus paper. Plastered on the front was a picture of me speaking on stage with the headline: "Mississippi State Alum Shares Her Story of Discrimination." The article went on to focus on my story about how I was treated by the Fellowship of Christian Athletes after I came out.

The overall response was outstanding. My mom ended up getting a lot of phone calls. She was ready to be an open voice and advocate for families like ours and became one of my biggest supporters. We were soon invited to speak to many classes on campus together, including religion classes. People reached out to her to say, "Hey, my sister is gay," or, "Did you know that my brother/son is gay?" People wanted to connect on a long-ignored subject in our small Southern town. They wanted someone who would understand to hear them. My mom approached each conversation with compassion and a wide-open heart. She gave people space to voice their own struggles and fears, which in return allowed her to process some of her own hurt and pain as well.

There is connection in vulnerability. Because I was vulnerable in my talk, others felt compelled to do the same. This openness was one of life's miracles that was waiting to be uncovered. But it didn't end there.

About three weeks after the event, I got a call from one of the directors of the Fellowship of Christian Athletes.

I was in my office when our assistant handed me the phone. A man said, "Hey, Meagan. I just wanted to call and tell you that I am real sorry about what you went through with the FCA. That's not what we are about, and I want to apologize on behalf of our organization. How about we get together and chat?"

I nearly dropped the phone. *Is this real?* I replied, "It was a very painful time for me, so your apology means more than you know."

After I hung up, all I felt was gratitude and humility. I felt gratitude because I realized I was in a place to let the apology in, and humility because I had waited for that moment for so long without knowing I had been waiting for it. I thought to myself, *This is why I was born.* It had never been clearer that I was meant to speak, meant to stand in my truth, meant to show up and be a gentle voice in a polarized world.

I had never expected an apology. I had never dreamt of an apology. But I had always hoped that we could somehow build a bridge between the gay community and the more conservative Christian community in Mississippi. In this instance, because we were both willing to be vulnerable, a conversation was born.

When I got to the ministry leader's office building, he met me at the door and led me down a long corridor that felt cold and stiff. When we arrived at his office, he turned around as light from the hallway beamed down on his pale skin. "Welcome," he said. He motioned for me to walk into his office but then hesitated and stuck out his hand to shake mine. I refused. I opened my arms to imply a hug, and he met me there.

I walked into his office, and he swept in behind me with high energy, plopping down in the chair behind his desk.

Our chat began with the basics—where are you from, how did you get to where you are, and so on. His energy was bubbly but calm, and mine was calm and reserved. He told me about his life, his faith, his faults, and his story, and I told him mine.

His intention for the talk was to be able to apologize to me face to face, and that is what he did. He went on to ask me, "Meagan, how can I love you more?" Meaning, "How can I, a conservative Christian, love you, a gay woman?" I was a bit frazzled by his offer. No one had asked me that before. I was silent for a moment to make sure I was connecting with my heart and not with my fear.

"What broke my heart when I came out of the closet is that people stopped seeing me for who I really was," I explained.

I told him that growing up I had been very focused on what I had wanted out of life. I had always known who I was. I played sports, made good grades, had a small group of really good friends, and spent most of my free time writing about spirituality and God. I was crushed that people assumed I didn't love God anymore or that I had forgotten who God was. I had found more of God when I found myself.

As a part of the Fellowship of Christian Athletes, I got a spiritual outlet in the only way I knew to get it. There weren't a lot of options I knew of at the time, so that group was my spiritual community—until I came out of the closet.

I continued, "That safe haven turned against me. It was as though who I was had been forgotten or misplaced, or even as if I had never existed. Deep down I always knew life was on my side, and I was determined to hold onto that belief even though I was being rejected at the time."

He shook his head and was silent, so I continued, "I stopped being seen. I just wanted to be seen. We all deserve to be seen for who we really are."

He moved his finger from his chin and sat up. "That's powerful."

He went on to tell me a few stories about his family, and I told him a few about my athletic career and my work life. I went on to talk about my own challenges, and he shared his. I jumped into saying how I feel like we have to move beyond agreeing to disagree and find a place between us where we can let go of our attachments to right and wrong, how if we could meet in that space, there won't be a reason for apologies in the future or tears and suffering around the subject. Perhaps we could coexist and support one another in that.

It was a simple conversation—the beginning of further, deeper conversations that ended as quickly as they came. After meeting a few more times to chat, I got this overwhelming feeling that his ultimate goal was to mentor me. It wasn't something he said specifically. It was just a gut feeling. Our conversations kept turning back on me and what I might be struggling with and what my walk with God might be missing. It's as though he wanted to shepherd me back from my gay lifestyle into a God-pleasing straight one. He wasn't direct, which made it really hard to pinpoint, until our final encounter.

We met for coffee one day, and I asked him if he wanted to be a part of a project I was working on called "Beyond Labels." I was interviewing different people around Mississippi and asking them questions like, "When people look at you, how do you think they label you?" "What do you feel like you are judged for the most?" "What was the biggest turning point in your life?" "What is your strongest value?" "How do you want to change the world?" I posted each interview on my blog with a goal to show our similarities beyond our differences.

To that he said, "I don't want to be a part of some agenda you have."

He pulled back his chair as if he were angry at me and walked out of the coffee shop. I was flabbergasted. My only agenda was unity.

If that had happened to me years before, I would have hesitated more when considering making new connections with people who saw the world so differently from me. This time, as I sat at the table, I let the burning inside my chest reach my eyes quickly. When I walked outside, tears streamed down my face. I let myself feel the misunderstanding instead of stuffing it down. I didn't want to hold on to something that wasn't mine.

That was the last time we talked.

I was saddened by our interaction. Did he back away because our friendship was going to be made public through my project? Did he just not know what to do with me? I brought love to the spaces we entered, and I truly wanted to bridge the gap. What was I missing?

I don't recall feeling like I had done anything that wasn't true for me. I was myself. I gave my heart, and that's all I could do. Other people's responses are not my responsibility.

CHAPTER 16

Clare and I climbed into bed one night when she softly asked me, "Are you ready to get married?"

Her warmth permeated the space. I curled my backside up against her body, inviting her to wrap her arms around me. I was silent. I'm always silent when something hits me hard.

It was soon after my National Coming Out Day experience. There was something about being on stage that day that had made me feel more confident in myself.

As we laid in bed, Clare asked me again, "Are you ready to get married?" I shrugged my shoulders and pushed closer to her. She didn't force the issue, and instead she just held me tighter. *I want to get married. I am so scared.* A few tears dropped onto my pillow, making me sniffle. "Are you crying?" she asked. I shook my head yes. She knew that meant I was working through something and just let me feel what I was feeling.

I didn't give Clare an answer that night. We fell asleep before speaking another word. I decided to mull it over for a few days.

We knew we wanted to get married, but Clare was waiting on me to be ready. Something was shifting in me, and I needed a chance to think about the idea and what that would entail. Getting married could be like another coming out experience, and I wasn't sure if I was strong enough to handle it.

Although Clare and I were "in a relationship" on social media, introducing her to new people as my partner had been a struggle for me. I usually liked to measure someone up to see if I thought they would be "cool" with it or not. I slowly began to see that wasn't fair to me, to them, or to Clare. Every day, I felt like I had to talk up my courage to be myself in the world. I was really tired of prepping, tired of worrying. I felt stuck, and I didn't want to be anymore.

I wondered if marriage would help me get over the wall I kept slamming into. I wondered even more why it was always such a challenge for me to be real.

Consciously putting my shield down and believing in myself and in the best of others became the cry of my heart. But when society, or when I believe that society (here in the South) is against who I am, it's tough to see the light in each person, to let them into my world without wanting to run and hide. When you're so used to lying about who you are, lying becomes a habit. Even then, I knew telling the truth was my only choice, but I have to admit that sometimes it was easier to say no to social events than to be uncomfortable. It was too painful to not tell the whole truth.

The Supreme Court hearings in 2013 stirred up something in me. When someone asked me, "Are you married?" it was always easier to tell them I wasn't rather than explain, "No, but only because I can't," which could have led to a richer conversation and a deeper connection. By then, Clare and I had been together for over five years and had every intention of getting married. In fact, we were married in our own way. We were as official as we legally could be. When I would tell people I wasn't married, I felt defeated, I felt like a liar, and I felt like I was choosing the easy way out, which made it easy to spiral into self-defeat.

The weekend before the hearings, Clare and I went to get haircuts. There was a total of five of us there in the salon, and we were all making small talk. A woman I didn't know was getting ready to leave, and she asked me if Clare and I were friends or sisters. I took a run around my head first, which told me to be completely honest.

"No, actually, Clare is my partner."

I felt confident. I felt liberated. I felt like there was nothing to apologize for because there wasn't. We are who we are.

The woman casually remarked, "Oh, okay," and went on to ask questions about sports. It didn't matter that she wasn't enamored with our relationship. What mattered was that I didn't feel the need to explain myself. I didn't feel that deep dark hole of doubt creeping in. I felt victorious. However, I have to admit that I think there's something wrong when just answering a simple question becomes such a victory.

After that interaction, I wondered why getting to this point had been such a difficult feat for me. Put me on NPR, and I will tell you my story of coming out in Mississippi. Put me on TV, and I will talk with a Baptist preacher about being gay in Mississippi. Put me in front of a crowded room—no problem, I'm gay and proud (and nervous). But one-on-one? That's a completely different story. That's when shame or fear invades my vocal cords and the words I speak aren't lies, but they aren't the truth either.

Was all of it my fault? Was my internal struggle of acceptance something I did to myself? I began articulating what had been bothering me for a long time. I knew Mississippi wasn't packed full of a victorious progressive history, but I was choosing to live here, so shouldn't I have been taking the blame? No, at least not completely. I realized I was just as responsible as everyone else.

I saw clearly that for us all to experience love and acceptance, it was going to take me continuing to have the courage to be truthful in those one-on-one conversations, and it was going to take a lot more people like my dad speaking matter-of-factly about Clare being my partner. It was going to take courage on my part to grab Clare's hand in public when I felt compelled and not let go when someone looked our way.

What I was going through around my fears of getting married led me to write a blog post. This post helped me work through my internal struggle to identify and overcome my hesitancy about marriage:

The thought of getting married terrifies me—not because I don't want to get married. It's just all the fears that come with the thought of it. Will everyone truly want to be there and not feel weird about it? Will I feel awkward and uncomfortable? I know I am gay, but I am still sifting through whether I "deserve" a wedding day or not. And let's be honest, having a ceremony where it isn't legal and may not be for a while isn't that appealing (even though I definitely know I would want it to be in Mississippi).

And the fears carry on: Am I ready to fully be me at such a ceremony? Will people be excited when I tell them I am getting married? Or will they have no response at all, or "okay" and head nod responses, or just be uncomfortable? Will I have to be careful who I invite because they may not "agree" with my choice to get married? Should there be a kiss at the ceremony? A hug? It feels like coming out again—preparing for the worst, slightly hoping for the best, while still knowing deep down that incredible outcomes are possible . . .

The thought of telling my family and friends I want to get married makes me sick to my stomach. I can't bear the thought of possibly going through what I have been through before . . . Deep down, when I think of telling others I am getting married, I feel the need to beg, "Please support me. Please support me. Don't hurt me with your words or lack thereof. Don't tell me you don't agree but you'll support me anyway. Don't tell me you don't understand and that you won't come because your faith is more important to you. Don't do it. Please just support me and love me. Please just be excited, and let's celebrate!"

As I have been evaluating my process, I am very aware of my fears while still holding on to the dream of having a ceremony of some sort. I realize a few things standing in my way that I am ready to let go of. Above the doorway to my dream is a sign that says "Forgiveness." I may appear to be someone who is able to let go easily, but I am not. At the same time, I understand and trust that my process is unique to me and it *is necessary for it to be as it is. I acknowledge I have held on to being looked down upon by the majority of our society. It is embedded so deeply, even though things are in the midst of changing. I have allowed others' beliefs to seep into my own and have been yanking at the seams of breaking open and showing my full self.*

A wedding would be that for me: a full expression of who I am—all of my vulnerability, every bit of my courage, every ounce of trust that I have, and my willingness to get hurt by fully putting myself out there to be looked upon, to be loved in a new way, and to ultimately accept myself. It will take all of me to do it, and it will take all of those around me. In order to welcome all to take part in my dream, I know I must forgive the past—the past that remains inside of me. And I will continue to forgive over and over... and over—including forgiving myself for all the times when I just couldn't muster up the courage to fully be who I am.

When I first started sharing, I thought it was for other people, but it became the path for my own healing.

PART III

CONNECT

Connecting isn't about changing others. It's about opening the door. The best way to open that door is through vulnerability.

CHAPTER 17

Rubbing my eyes, I rolled over slowly to face Clare in bed and quietly told her, "I'm ready to get married."

She swiftly opened her eyes as if she were in disbelief and asked, "Are you sure?"

"Yeah." She jumped over to my side of the bed and squished me with excitement.

"You know you have to tell your family first," she said. I nuzzled my head into her body to hide my face. I started to pout and pulled Clare closer to avoid getting out of bed.

I knew I was strong and confident enough to embark on this journey with her, but announcing that we were getting married was nerve-racking. I began replaying my coming out day in my mind and wondered if I could handle any reaction that might come our way. I worried I might feel less than again or that people would tell me they loved me but didn't agree with gay marriage or that I might feel responsible for my family's reactions, whether good, bad, or indifferent.

I never thought the day would come when I would be ready to get married. It wasn't because I didn't want to. I was just terrified. As much as I knew I had come a long way and worked hard to move on from the messages I'd told myself when I came out of the closet the first time, I was afraid those messages—I am a failure, I am not good enough, I am not okay as I am, I am less than—would seep in again, or more accurately, that I would let them in and believe them again.

I decided to be patient with my worries and allow myself enough space and time to be ready to get married, and then the day came.

I huffed and puffed over telling the first few family members, as I knew that would be the hardest—not because their reactions would be negative, but because I was overcoming something. Looking back, I feel like I was finding myself in a whole new way. Marriage was something I wanted so deeply, but I had told myself I couldn't have it for so long that on some level, I didn't think it could actually happen. As a result, its meaning had slipped from my fingertips as I longed to be like the next straight couple who could easily jump through the traditional hoops laid before them. I didn't think I wanted to get married as a gay person. I'd told myself it wasn't important.

I pulled my parents into my new office.

"I have something I want to tell you."

They both froze for a moment before they pulled my niece into my office and closed the door behind them. My mom's face turned a shade whiter, and my dad started tapping his foot on the ground in anticipation.

"We want to get married in New York."

I didn't mention to Clare that I was going to tell them, but why suffer in another closet when I had good news? Holding things in at that point seemed useless, but my mom was unprepared. "What do you mean? How will you get married in New York?"

I was deflated by her response. It took me back to when I told her I was gay. "It's legal in New York. We are ready to get married."

She blurted back, "You need to tell your brothers before you tell anyone else."

That's odd, I thought. I think she could tell that I was hurt from her direct, fearful reaction. My dad reached for my arm, pulled me toward him, and said, "Congratulations. I am so happy for you. That's great news."

My mom snapped out of her state of worry, and her energy shifted to excitement.

"We are going to New York!"

That's more like it. As I walked them out of my office, I received at least a hundred more hugs from my mom as if her hopes and dreams for me were coming true too.

After telling the rest of my family, I realized how deeply the desire to do so was embedded in my dreams. Once I expressed it, once I realized I could have my heart's desire, I was surprised at my joy and sense of liberation. My state of mind about myself, the world, and the way I felt about magic shifted. If you are patient, if you listen, if you follow your heart, you will eventually experience the joy that comes from suffering.

By embracing myself, life embraced me. The Universe was supporting me as I actively went after what my heart wanted, and a sense of safety started weaving its way into my perception.

As we told more and more people we were getting married, their reactions were above and beyond my expectations, and any discomfort I had had with the idea settled with each new response. Clients sent us flowers, friends posted their excitement on Facebook, and people threw engagement parties for us.

Even so, the idea of getting married to a woman was still an adjustment for me. Years of cultural shaming played a part, I am sure, but it seemed as though it was not an adjustment for anyone else—just natural and genuine enthusiasm. They all confirmed what I had known deep down was possible. I had just never dared to dream I would actually see the day when I would feel such love in my heart coming in from the world outside of me. It wasn't that it had never tried to get in before. The difference was I was finally letting it in.

Leading up to getting married, I developed a strong meditation practice to help me cope with the fears I had coming up. I would always find myself visualizing standing with Clare, encircled by our loved ones as they poured their love and support into the moment. I can't say I remember specific faces. It was more of a feeling that transcended my everyday experiences. It was the same feeling I'd felt when I was with Desiree years earlier and felt connected to everything and everyone around me. Its power was so overwhelming that when I would immerse myself in it, I felt connected to the bigness of love. It was clear I was a part of it, and every time I was moved to tears because there was no better way to express that kind of adoration. Each time after meditating, I thought, *I wonder if I will ever get to experience this vision in this life.*

I've never felt as free as I did on my wedding weekend. My own confidence was a surprise to me, as I thought I would be more self-conscious. I was self-conscious, but I was constantly pushing that part of me away. I was mostly nervous about kissing Clare in public, let alone in front of fifty other familiar faces. Public displays of affection have never been my thing. While I have been accepting of myself on one level, I have always felt challenged by displaying any sort of affection toward Clare in public. I am not talking about making out, but simple, loving gestures that imply we are a couple. If Clare and I are holding hands in our car in Mississippi and we stop next to another vehicle at a stop light that could *possibly* look in our direction and see us holding hands, I let go. But something changed inside of me on my wedding weekend. I found myself reaching for Clare's hand in the crowds of Manhattan and putting my arm around her in front of my family and friends, a welcomed surprise.

I could feel the entire group of folks who had made the trip to New York stretching and growing with me. No one had ever had an experience like ours before, so I welcomed their questions and curiosity. The night before the wedding my cousin asked what we were going to be wearing for the ceremony. I answered, "White."

He then said, "Well, I've never done this before, so I don't know what to expect."

"Me neither."

We had no specific rules or traditions to follow, so we made them up as we went along, and it all somehow magically fell into place as if it had already been written. The unknown details of my dream were unfolding right in front of me.

When I woke up the morning of our wedding day, the nerves started rolling in. Clare went off to hang out with her family. As I was walking the city streets to meet my family, I popped my earbuds in and started listening to piano music. It soothed me as I took in the smells of the city. The anticipation of the morning rush was around me, and my nerves were working their way out with every step down the New York asphalt.

After lunch, my mom met Clare and me in our hotel room to help us get ready for the ceremony. My mom laid out my white sequined blouse and white linen pants on the bed. We didn't exchange words while she applied my makeup and fixed my hair. She glowed like most mothers of the bride were supposed to. She handed me my blouse and then my pants. Once I stood up and faced her, she said, "You look beautiful."

Through each part of the process, I found a new part of myself. With joy and anticipation, I consciously watched each moment float by. Appreciation and gratitude protected me from any self-doubt. I was deeply touched by those who had traveled to be with us and overwhelmed with gratitude for those who had paved the way to make our marriage possible. I felt both infinitesimal and expansive at the same time.

Once we were ready, we caught a cab and picked up Clare's dad (our officiant and a retired Episcopal bishop) and his wife on our way to where we would be meeting everyone else for the ceremony: the Sixth Avenue entrance to Central Park. When we arrived, we were greeted by half our party, took pictures, and signed our marriage license. As we waited for everyone to arrive, an old childhood friend took on the responsibility of finding us a spot in the park. She immediately happened upon one of the most popular wedding sites just fifty yards from where we were standing, and it was available.

The clouds hovered above us. They had been threatening rain all day but had yet to follow through. However, the smell of rain was near. Once everyone arrived, we made our way up a steep hill toward the beautiful gazebo covered with greenery. The hill reminded me of my own journey of climbing one step at a time away from fear and toward my inner freedom. It was then when we found ourselves hedged in by a circle of those we loved.

During each pause, I looked around at the eyes surrounding me, taking it in . . . letting it in. My eyes were filled with tears throughout the service. My dad read from 1 Corinthians, Clare's dad spoke on love and equality, we read our vows to one another and exchanged rings, and as Clare's dad was saying the final blessing and final words, "What God has joined together let no man put asunder" (Matthew 19:6), it began to rain upon our union. My mom stepped up behind me and sheltered Clare, me, and her dad with her umbrella. She put her arm around me as we all said the "Our Father" along with everyone else in attendance.

That prayer had never meant so much to me as it did that day, not because of its words, but because of the unity it sparked. After the prayer, Clare's dad asked us to seal our commitment with a kiss. For once, I didn't pause to ponder the possible consequences of kissing a woman in public. I chose truth without hesitation and was instantly uncuffed from the shackles of my past.

We went on to have a magnificent celebration full of toasts, laughter, dancing, and love. I'll never forget a moment of my wedding day.

Returning to Mississippi as a married woman was tougher than I thought it would be. Introducing Clare as my wife was a new challenge that forced me to let go of more fear and experience new levels of freedom. It was part of my healing process that was supported by my circle of love. All the while, my wholeness had been quietly waiting for me to choose my truth.

CHAPTER 18

I was pacing outside of City Hall, waiting for my dad to arrive. I asked him to walk in with me because I wanted his safe presence around when I gave the speech of my life.

He pulled up in his blue work truck, walked toward me with a warm, fatherly aura, put his arms around me, and asked, "Are you okay?"

I shrugged.

"You can do this."

I didn't feel like I could do anything. He escorted me in and made me feel like I could get through what was about to happen. In 2018, two college students applied for a permit for Starkville to have its first Pride parade. When I heard the news, I jumped in to help with planning and finding a way to bridge the business and college communities. Having a parade was a sure sign our city was making progress, and that excited me, but I was still nervous about what the overall response was going to be.

Even though Mississippi State is in Starkville, it often feels like the two are in separate worlds. The city often functions on its own with its own events, and the university does the same.

The first permit was voted down by the city council, which sent everyone into a flurry. The unapproved parade was the topic of the town and eventually received national press. The students decided to threaten the city with a lawsuit, which put the permit decision back on the table.

The LGBTQ+ community asked me to speak on their behalf. Before my name was called, we all sat and listened to opposing sides argue back and forth about the topic of the day. I sat shaking in my seat the entire time. My body was quivering inside while others fanned their faces with their ruffled council agendas. Clare was sitting to my left and my parents to my right. Clare kept rubbing my back, and my mom patted my knee in reassurance.

There were hundreds of people in attendance—inside and outside—watching, listening, and waiting for the decision. I was the last to speak.

The speaker before me spoke about gay marriage being a sin and that she wouldn't have a Pride parade in her town damaging the youth. My stomach turned a few more times as I tried not to let her words affect me.

The mayor introduced me when it was my turn to approach the podium.

"From the LAMBDA professionals group, please welcome our next speaker, Meagan O'Nan."

I grabbed my script. My knees were weak as I took the stage. I placed my papers on the podium and couldn't keep my hands from trembling. I looked at the panel to find faces of many different colors. To my right was a man I grew up with, who I had been friends with, who was vehemently against gay rights. On the rest of the panel were our newly elected progressive mayor, two city council members who had never made eye contact with me when I had spoken on previous occasions, and two other men who were more open-minded, although one was undecided on his stance.

I glanced at each person before I began.

My voice broke, so I cleared my throat and began again.

"When I was preparing for this speech, I got stuck. I knew I didn't want to address the Bible, and I knew I didn't want to address the law. We have been circling these two topics for years now, and the only progress we have made is causing more division and hurt feelings. Everyone thinks they are right and that the other side is wrong. This is the great human divide."

I glanced up to see only three sets of eyes staring back at me.

"When I was feeling stuck, my mom called me. I told her I was struggling with what to say and how to say it. She went on to remind me of the most important things—that we are all afraid of being rejected, that we have all been hurt, and that we all want to be accepted."

I looked back at my mom, who looked like she was holding her breath. I stood taller.

"Gay. Straight. Christian. Buddhist. Agnostic. Republican. Democrat. Jewish. White. Black. Sikh. Hindu. Native American. Rich. Poor. Female. Male. Transgender. Taoist. Immigrant. Mormon. Muslim. Atheist. The list could go on and on. These are our community members. We all have different labels, but we all want the same thing: to be loved and accepted.

"The challenge we all face is how to love and accept one another when the going gets tough—when we feel hurt, when we feel scared, when we feel like we aren't being heard, when we are afraid of what everyone else is going to think of us. To be honest, being up here right now and putting myself out there—I'm scared. These feelings aren't new to me. Being a person who is gay isn't easy. Being gay sets you up for being completely misunderstood.

"The reality of our world is that hate crimes have drastically risen since 2015, and the reality of our world is that our children are killing themselves and each other. There is deep hurt and deep sadness among us. Exclusion is the culprit for the violence in the world. Decisions that are being made by our elected officials, they disconnect us from each other and either make us feel less than or more than. Neither way works.

"Is the decision to deny the LGBTQ community a Pride parade really a big deal? Yes. It tells one part of our community that they are less than, and it tells another part of our community that they are more than.

"According to the CDC, LGBTQ youth seriously contemplate suicide at almost three times the rate of heterosexual youth. LGBTQ youth are almost five times as likely to have attempted suicide compared to heterosexual youth. And in a national study, 40 percent of transgender adults reported having made a suicide attempt, and 92 percent of these individuals reported having attempted suicide before the age of twenty-five."

The stats hit me hard the second I said them aloud. I was tasked with speaking up for people who needed a voice, people who needed to be understood, and I felt the weight of that responsibility.

"So, why do we want a Pride parade? Because our community is at risk. Lives are at risk. The LGBTQ community needs to know that they are worthy, that they are loved, and that they are accepted. The intention of the parade is to celebrate who we are.

"As a person who is gay, you spend your life hiding—doing everything you can to avoid letting people know who you are. And when it gets to a point that it hurts too much to hide, then you must dig deep to find enough confidence to be bold enough to be yourself. It's a daily struggle."

My voice broke as I pushed back my tears.

"To grab my wife's hand in public or not . . . It's a question that goes through my mind every day. Sometimes I am brave enough and don't care what other people think, and other times I just can't muster up the courage. Something as simple as holding a hand . . . another human's hand . . . can be so tough for so many.

"Several weeks ago, I heard a seven-year-old child call gay people disgusting. The one thing I heard that hurt me the most after I came out was being called disgusting. It's a horrible thing to say about another human being. Now, who did that child learn that from, that gay people are disgusting? They learned it from an adult.

"Every decision we make, every word we speak matters. I believe that we are all one, that we are all connected. What you do affects me, and what I do affects you. That's why I have spent my entire journey asking myself, how can I do better? How can I love better?"

I paused for a moment to catch my breath, and someone from the back of the room screamed, "Go Meagan!" I got a surge of energy.

"If you aren't gay, you will never understand. Just like I will never understand what it is like to be Black or transgender or a conservative Christian. I can't understand. But that doesn't mean that I get to deny you and that you get to deny me. We must reach deeper into our souls and find a way to value connection over a lack of understanding.

"The decision to not allow a Pride parade in Starkville doesn't make me any less gay, and it certainly isn't going to quiet my voice or make me want to move. But what it does is tell an important and special part of our community that they—that we—don't matter."

I looked back at my parents and pointed to them in the audience.

"When I first told my parents I was gay, their greatest fear was how I was going to be treated by others. Both of my parents are here tonight to support me. I have incredible parents. When I hurt, they hurt. They have seen firsthand how decisions like this hurt someone like me. They know the pain. They have lived it with me. Being gay doesn't just affect me; it affects my family and my friends. My mom always told me, 'Love yourself.' Just love yourself. Isn't that what we are all trying to do—love who we are?

"Our challenge as a human being is always how to love in the face of fear. How to love when we will never understand why someone is the way they are. We often choose fear over love because fear gives us the illusion of control, and love . . . love sets us up to be hurt, again. But love—love is the only part of who we are that allows us to experience the greatness of what it means to be human.

"In my world, in my bubble, I am surrounded by support and encouragement all the time. My company's motto is, 'People are good.' And I believe that with my entire heart. I see it every day. I believe that if you look for good, you will find it. And I see a lot of good that could come out of this entire situation. Perhaps we could all choose to come together: to heal, to let go, to accept, to forgive.

"None of those are easy things to do. It's a commitment. There has to be a willingness. We have to connect. We have to look in each other's eyes and see the humanity in others. There is no other way. It's that simple.

"I would love the opportunity to love you—everyone on this panel... everyone in this room. But you have to let me. And I have to let you. I am willing to do that. Even if it means I may get hurt, again.

"I hope that one day we can all walk together hand in hand. I hope that one day we won't care whose hand we are holding or whose hand another person is holding. I hope for that. I believe in that. Some people call me idealistic. But I don't care. I'd rather be idealistic than not. I'd rather hope for what I know is possible than to feel defeated by limitation.

"Every morning, I wake up. I journal. I work out. I meditate and pray. I take care of my spirit. Because I want to go out into the world with the purpose of making others feel loved. Especially since I have lived through so many times of not being seen or loved. To repeat what has been done to me is to continue the cycle of discrimination. And I refuse. I refuse to do that. So I will keep hoping. I will keep believing in the best of who we are and who we could be. Because I choose that.

"One of my personal heroes, Archbishop Desmond Tutu, writes, 'Is there a place where we can meet? You and me. The place in the middle. Where we straddle the lines. Where you are right. And I am right too. And both of us are wrong and wronged. Can we meet there? And look for the place where the path begins. The path that ends when we forgive.' Can we show the rest of the world how a community can come together in the face of turmoil and confusion? Can we show each other that we respect and honor one another, fairly and equally? Can we let go of the need to understand before we decide if we can love or not? Can we rise above our need to be right so that we can connect?

"We need peace in this world. We need forgiveness in this world. We need real connection. We welcome you and everyone to walk with us on March 24. Our arms are open."

The crowd roared as I walked away from the podium. The mayor was forced to get them to hush even though she was beaming with pride. I sat down in between my mom and my wife and was engulfed by their love. The feeling of safety had been achieved by showing up and speaking my truth.

The city council went immediately into the vote. The ones who had said no before said no again. And the ones who said yes before said yes again. That left one vote for the city council member who was on the fence. He conceded his vote, and it was left to the mayor.

He didn't want to be the one who said yes, so he let her do it. The mayor voted, "Yea."

The room burst with pride. My heart filled with hope.

When Pride Parade Day came, I wasn't prepared for how it would make me feel. There were so many years when I felt inferior and invisible. To suddenly feel validated by those in my own community, a community that once didn't stand by my side, was life changing.

Clare and I led the parade with the other organizers, holding hands and waving at all of those standing in the streets who were cheering and waving and running over to hug us. With over three thousand people in attendance, something shifted for me that day. The warmth and support from the onlookers were like a warm blanket. Even as protestors shouted in the background, their voices were just another part of the symphony of our humanity. I walked on and smiled deep within.

The speech and the parade were turning points for me. I was ready to move on to the next chapter of my life. It was time to take a break from advocacy and rest and start the family I had always wanted. It was time for me to relish in my inner freedom and choose a life based on my dreams and not on the limiting beliefs I had placed on myself for so many years.

CHAPTER 19

Clare entered the room with a syringe full of sperm while I waited on our bed. The feeling of having a man's sperm inside my body was repulsive but necessary to get what I wanted.

I sat there for thirty minutes with my legs in the air, hoping for the right result so I wouldn't have to do this again.

I had always wanted my own family and a daughter named Merit. My middle name is Merit, and I had always hoped that my parents would have chosen to give me that name as my first name. My great-grandmother's middle name was also Merit, and she was such a special and kind soul. I've aspired to be like her my whole life. The name Merit has always meant so much to me.

I shelved the idea of having a baby for a long time because I couldn't see how I, a gay woman, could have a family. I had no models to look up to, marriage wasn't legal at the time, and where in the world would the sperm come from? Judging by the religious teachings of my youth, immaculate conception was an option but highly unlikely. I had no clue where this dream of mine would take me, or if it were even possible.

The way I met Clare after calling out to the Universe is the same way gears fell into motion for having a daughter almost four years later. There was a moment in 2012 when, in my heart of hearts, I knew without a doubt I would have my daughter. Whether through my body or adoption, she would come into my life at the right time. In fact, I wrote a letter to her that day, and the same feelings and desire I had when I spoke to God about wanting a partner were there again.

Dear Merit, I know you are out there. I know you will make your way to me. I feel like you are already a part of my life and that I am just waiting to lay my eyes on you. I love you more than you know. However you decide to find your way into my life won't matter to me. I just want you, my dear daughter.

I believe your heart always knows what it truly wants, and when you decide you are ready for it and say it out loud, the Universe starts moving mountains right then and there to make it so. It's our job to let go of how we think it should look, let it come in its own time, and spend our time allowing ourselves to feel deserving of whatever the dream may be. That's the tough part.

I never imagined I'd move back to Mississippi with one hundred dollars in my pocket and a woman fifteen years older than me. But I did. I never imagined I would have the opportunity to get married to that same woman. But I did. In the same way, I never imagined I would have the opportunity to have a child.

After we got married, Clare and I thought about adoption for a few years, but the laws in Mississippi made it impossible for us. After fostering a dog, I knew I couldn't ever foster a child. To love someone unconditionally with the possibility of having them taken away was a risk I didn't want to take. We tried a sperm bank for a while, but that got expensive and too hard to plan for, so we took a break and waited. In fact, I pretty much gave up after that. We asked a few guy friends along the way if they would help, but nothing ever panned out.

And then there was our friend Josh.

We had come to love him over the years. It dawned on us one day that he would be the perfect man to ask to donate sperm so we could expand our family. While he was in our office one day for acupuncture, Clare decided to have the conversation with him without me. I was afraid he would say no, so I didn't want to be there.

As I was waiting nervously in my office for an answer, Clare rushed in and shouted, "He said yes!"

She was jumping up and down. I stood up and jumped up and down with her. I couldn't believe it was happening. Not only was he fully committed to donating his sperm, he was also fully committed to being in our child's life, which was exactly what we wanted.

When we began trying to get pregnant, Josh would come to our house when I was ovulating (sometimes three to four times in a span of four to five days), go into our bathroom, and come out with sperm in a jar. Clare would put it into a syringe and insert it. Then we'd wait.

Six months of trying had led to nothing, until one day when I felt off. A few weeks before, I had started feeling nauseous. I bought a pregnancy test, but I didn't want to get too hopeful. When I peed on the stick, the double pink lines popped up almost immediately.

Clare and I hugged each other tightly, then put on some music and had a dance party. We couldn't wait to share the news.

I'll never forget our parents' reactions. Clare's dad was still alive at the time. We video-called him, and all we could see were his nose hairs on the screen. We told him we had news, and he joyfully shouted, "It worked!"

My mom cried tears of disbelief when we told her. The euphoria was unreal. I could not believe this was happening to me. It was the best day of my life.

Even so, I still had fears about becoming a parent, most of which centered around being a gay parent. How would the staff treat us at our OB-GYN's office? How would they treat us at the hospital? If we were to seek care for Merit at a religious daycare center, would they let us in? How would Merit, having two mothers, fare with kids her own age? Would life be extra hard for her? What if I lost the baby? Or what if she got here and I outlived her? And oh my god, how in the hell was I going to get this baby out of that tiny hole?

Fears or no fears, this baby was on the way, and she was going to do whatever she was going to do.

On the night of November 7, 2018, I returned home from a dinner with Clare and our moms. I was feeling much heavier than usual and could barely walk to the car without losing my breath. I was due on the tenth, so we knew labor was near. Sure enough, around midnight that night, my mucus plug came out, and the contractions started coming.

I labored at home with the support of Clare, my mom, and our doula until the contractions became too intense. Once we were at the hospital, the doctor had to break my water for fear I would be too tired to give birth if we didn't move it along. I was fully dilated fairly quickly after that. It was time to push.

After four hours of pushing and an excruciating twenty-two hours of labor, I was beyond fatigued. I'd been up for forty hours, and we were getting nowhere. The doctor recommended a C-section, which was the last thing I had wanted. After all that work, Merit wasn't even crowning. I felt like a failure.

The next thirty minutes were the worst. The announcement of the C-section didn't stop the contractions from coming every other minute. I was scared. I was crying. I was exhausted. And Clare was there through every single moment, holding my hand, massaging my back, and cheering me on.

At 10:30 p.m. on November 8, we got to hear our baby girl cry for the first time. I was full of morphine, but I will never forget that sound or the feeling of Clare by my side as our daughter took her first breath. I wondered what she looked like, and part of me was concerned. Just the day before, I had gotten a sonogram that made her lips look enormous. As they walked Merit across the room to check her, I could see her from a distance. She was the most beautiful soul I had ever seen. After I took my first glance at her in person, I turned to Clare and asked, "Are her lips okay? I can't tell."

Her lips were fine.

They finally brought Merit to me, and I talked to her and kissed her and touched her. It was like looking at myself in the mirror. Her dark hair, her blue eyes, the curve of her face—everything was familiar about her. It didn't feel real, but she was real. She was here.

Nothing compares to becoming a parent. All of a sudden, you can see your heart living outside of your chest. It's not safe like your heart living inside your body, and so the lessons of letting go happen in every moment. I became keenly aware of her breath and kept making sure she was still breathing. If she slept too long, I wondered if she was okay. Every moment meant letting go in some way. I had to let her be, but I also had to protect her, which was both hard and freeing.

I finally understood my mom's fear for me when I came out of the closet and her impulse to hold me close, protect me, and keep me from harm.

For the first hour of Merit's life, I was alone in recovery from our C-section. Luckily, Clare was holding her skin to skin the whole time. It was the slowest hour of my life, and it didn't help that I was exhausted and high. The staff were talking to me to keep me awake when all I wanted them to do was leave me alone, give me my baby, and let me fucking sleep. When I finally made it back to my room, everyone was there waiting. It was my turn for skin to skin with Merit. I was in awe. She latched on immediately to my nipple, and our special journey began.

Even now, I still can't believe she is here. Every time I put her down for bed at night, I say to her, "I can't wait to see you in the morning." And I mean it every single time.

As for my fears of how we would be treated at the hospital, the OB-GYN and his office staff were incredible with us. They even wanted us to bring the baby over to their clinic after she was born so they could meet her. They all gathered around us when we got there. Their love and care meant the world to us. We still keep in touch with two of the nurses who worked with us. They treated us like queens all the way through the process, and I will be forever grateful.

As for Josh, he doesn't have parental rights. He signed those away after Merit was born, and Clare is the other parent on her birth certificate. He even gave up coffee while we were going through the process because it was supposed to help elevate his sperm count. We are so very lucky to have our friend who gave us the most precious gift anyone could ever receive.

The process of making Merit was a journey I was fully committed to, no matter how it looked. I wanted a daughter as badly as I wanted to breathe. Those are the dreams that deserve our attention. Pay attention, let go of how you think it should look, wait, and act when the time is right. And when the time does come and your dream is staring at you in your eyes, it will be better than you ever imagined.

Not only is Merit a healthy and energetic three-year-old, but she is also surrounded by my parents, Clare's mom, aunts, uncles, and cousins. Josh's family lives nearby, and she gets all of that love as well. Our greater community loves her, and they have been a big part of her story. I certainly never imagined that—especially from a community that once rejected me.

I always pictured Merit, but I never pictured it this way. Not with all of this extra love.

I don't know what Merit's journey will be, but I know that mine is complete because of her. So far, she loves life, and she loves people. We will teach her what we have learned ourselves: that life is what you make it, your perception of yourself is what matters most, your value is embedded in your very existence, and that is enough. Love is always right there if you open your eyes and heart to it. And God is always by your side, guiding you back to your heart's desires.

All of this began with a dream and grew from a lot of hard work: rocky relationships, hard conversations, healing, forgiving, self-acceptance, and a willingness to let love in again.

I believe much of life will always be a mystery, but I know for sure that dreams do come true. And love? Love will always find its way to you when you are willing to let it in.

CHAPTER 20

Clare's hemoglobin was a four. Her blood pressure was 80/25. If she hadn't gone to the bathroom again, she would have died in her sleep. If I hadn't been awake, she would have died on the toilet.

As she lay in the hospital bed with someone else's blood dripping into her veins, I was aware of the care we weren't receiving. No one was running tests, and no one knew what was going on. All I wanted was my child in my arms and my family together at home, healthy.

I dropped my head onto Clare's lap. She rested, and I cried. I couldn't imagine my life without her. The veil between life and death was thin enough that I could sense God between us.

My chin quivered as I squeezed Clare's hand and whispered, "Please don't take her from me."

Fear has been paralyzing for me. Fear has been exhausting. I'm scared of losing the people I love the most.

Losing my friends in car accidents in high school set a precedent. I became mindful of every moment, knowing that in any given moment I could lose someone I love. Learning to be present is a valuable skill, but it is easy to allow fear to overtake any moment and turn it into all-encompassing worry that takes you down various paths of how that person's life could end quickly and forever.

I can be in a moment of complete bliss with my daughter while she is playing outside and suddenly get this gut-wrenching feeling she is going to jump into our lake and drown. And she isn't even near the lake.

I have come close to losing my wife twice in the last few years. She has had stomach issues off and on over the last ten years. We've tried everything to help her control the unpredictable pain. Right before Merit's first birthday, I went to Clare's office to check on her because she had been complaining of stomach pain. Her assistant said she was in the bathroom. I found her lying on the floor next to the toilet, passed out. I was in such shock that I picked her up and neglected to look at what was in the toilet. I vaguely remember blood, but I flushed it because the smell was unbearable. She woke up, and I took her home. We thought she had the stomach flu.

Each day, her skin was getting paler and paler. I noticed at one point that her lips had no color at all. After that, we agreed to go to the doctor the next morning. That night, she got up to go to the bathroom, and on her way back she called out to me to help her. As soon as I reached her, she passed out in my arms. When she came to, I put her in bed and lied awake, completely freaked out.

About an hour later, she got up to go to the bathroom again. This time, I walked with her. As she was sitting on the toilet, she passed out. I caught her. I pulled her off the toilet and noticed she wasn't breathing, panicked, grabbed my phone, and called 911. As I was talking to the operator, Clare began to breathe again. The ambulance arrived quickly, and I called my parents to watch Merit. The hospital was just a mile away, but it was the longest mile I had ever driven.

They determined Clare had a gastrointestinal bleed, but none of the providers ever found the cause. We sought out more tests and specialists, but still nothing.

We have a hunch it was a slow-bleeding ulcer that healed quickly. No matter the cause, we completely reevaluated our lives and decided it was most important to be with Merit as much as possible, to have the freedom to travel when we want, to work from home, to keep our stress as low as possible, and to deepen our relationships with friends and family.

We sold our ever-growing business we had worked hard to build for almost eight years because we knew the stress of managing a brick-and-mortar business was just too much for us at the time.

In February 2020, the same thing happened again, except this time, we were in a house that was further away from the hospital. We also caught it sooner than before. Clare passed out three times in less than five minutes.

I felt alone as she passed out in our bathroom while two-year-old Merit looked on. "Merit, go tell Nini to help. Run!"

I instructed her. She took off to get Clare's mom from the other side of the house.

Clare laid in my arms as her breath became shallow. *Not again. Not again. Please God, not again.*

I picked up her limp body and shuffled her across our house by her armpits to our car. "Nini, stay here with Merit. I am going to take Clare to the hospital myself."

Each time she passed out as I was carrying her, my heart broke at the thought the life I loved so much was slipping out of my hands. As I drove ninety miles per hour across town to the ER, I had a gut-wrenching feeling we weren't going to make it fast enough. My fears were loud. My hope was quiet.

I had to advocate for her life in the hospital that had misdiagnosed her before, which led me to getting in a fight with the ER doctor who wouldn't listen to me. For a whole week, we were in a hospital, scared for Clare's life as her blood counts continued to drop. This was the same hospital that had almost killed her last time. We had to wait to be transferred to a hospital that she would make it out of alive.

We were determined to get answers this time, but because this instance happened during COVID-19, finding proper care was nearly impossible. Our small Mississippi hospital was short on resources, and getting a transfer to a hospital with a GI doctor was difficult. I was beside myself for the three days we waited to get a transfer because Clare's hemoglobin numbers were slowly trickling down. We knew it was a GI bleed, but none of the professionals seemed to agree.

Once we found a spot in another hospital, the doctors discovered she had a duodenal ulcer that had burst as a result of *H. pylori,* all of which could be treated with antibiotics. When we got the results, we both hugged and cried tears of gratitude. I left that experience completely traumatized—grateful, but emotional and unsure about how our lives would look in the near future.

We've heard all our lives we can't have the life we want, that it's too hard, too risky, or too scary to go for it. Clare and I have never felt that way. We decided to continue creating the life we wanted. I saw Clare beginning to set boundaries with relationships that weren't serving her anymore. I saw her embrace herself in a new way. Her energy eased. It was almost like she hit the pause button on life and let things come to her instead of feeling like she had to go get them.

We decided to sell our house and move to a new home in the country on seven acres, something we had always wanted to do but hadn't acted on. I began to dive into my work again as Merit went off to daycare.

Clare's illnesses brought me to my knees many times. The thought of losing her forced me to think about what I would do if I were left behind with a young child and mother-in-law living with me. The thought of going through life without her left me desperate every time. It forced me so deep into my fears that I either had to evolve or crumble.

I chose to evolve.

I allowed myself to feel my feelings and move forward knowing that life is unpredictable and change will always be the only constant. I've shared my fears and our challenges with our community, which helped with my own healing.

As a gay woman, I've searched for safety over the years, and the appearance of safety has come in the form of those I love. I know it's false security because physical form never lasts. My light has been dimmed so much throughout my life, but the one thing I never want to dim is the love I have for my family. That's the God within me, which, it turns out, is the kind of love I have always been searching for to make me whole.

It's not a love that ever disappears. I get that now. I'd be heartbroken if I lost my wife or my daughter, but I know now that what they've given me is what I always believed was true: that God is within me and around me at all times.

CHAPTER 21

The fear that people won't see me for who I am still lingers today because it has been such a big part of my experience, but then I remember I am secure in myself and can handle rejection when it happens. I have seen enough and been through enough to know that anyone's lack of acceptance toward me isn't about me. Plus, I love me. I don't need anyone else's acceptance.

It's so easy to revert to past traumas. One of my favorite tools to kick myself back into the present is to ask myself, *Who do I want to be in this moment?* It always helps redirect me.

When we thought about having a baby, one of my fears was the kind of daycare she would receive. Most options in Mississippi are church based, but churches haven't always been a welcoming and accepting place for me or my family. In fact, we have chosen not to attend any church in our area because they are all Christian centered. We were looking for something inclusive of all faiths, like the community we had in Colorado.

I stayed home with Merit for the first two years of her life because I wanted to. I did so until January of 2021, when it became clear she needed more than just me. She needed to be challenged and socially active. We found a home daycare that she loved and thrived in. Sadly, the woman caring for Merit told us she would be moving that June. So, we had to begin our search for another daycare again.

Since the options were limited in our city, we had to give the church daycares a chance. When we drove up for a tour of one of them, the thought crossed my mind that Clare and I shouldn't tell them we were married. As quickly as the thought came in, it went out when I asked myself, *Who do I want to be in this situation?* Authentic, even if it meant rejection.

Upon arrival, one of the teachers asked Clare if she was Merit's grandmother (she gets that all the time), and Clare said, "No, I am her other mom." The woman laughed and apologized, bent down toward Merit, and said, "You are so lucky to have two moms."

Clare and I watched each other light up. We stood a little bit taller throughout the rest of the tour.

We didn't end up at that church daycare because they only had a part-time spot available, but a full-time spot came open for Merit at the public daycare that we also had a good experience with.

When Merit started, I still had fears about being accepted as a family, but Merit's need for social stimulation far outweighed my fears.

Clare and I didn't really run into her classmates' parents when we dropped Merit off or picked her up. Merit was thrilled with her school and her friends, so I felt like my fears were unreasonable, but they were real for me. I'd been afraid when the other parents found out Merit had two moms, they would encourage their children not to play with her.

Clare and I wanted to get to know the other parents and the other children, so we decided to invite everyone to our house for a potluck. We sent out invitations and signed them, "Merit's Two Moms."

We decided being authentic up front would make it easier for everyone. We weren't sure what the response would be, so we waited for the RSVPs.

I already knew one of Merit's classmate's moms, so that was comforting. We grew up playing basketball together in junior high and high school. Reconnecting with her was a huge relief for me. Every day I dropped Merit off, the two girls hugged and laughed like they didn't have a care in the world.

One by one, we got responses from the parents and learned there was another child in Merit's class who also had two moms. What were the chances in a small Mississippi town?

Not everyone showed up or responded to our invitation, but that didn't matter. More than half of them came. The kids ran in and out of the living room grabbing handfuls of popcorn and sipping their juice boxes. The parents laughed in the kitchen as we watched our diverse set of children play.

The freedom of the moment pierced my heart, and gratitude lifted the fog of my past traumas.

I'd learned, once again, that going for what you want is worth it, even when it's scary. Finding love I wouldn't otherwise have had is a risk I'm always willing to take.

We invite people into our home and into our lives so that we, as a family, can have rich experiences with all walks of life. Sharing myself and my stories over the years has led me to a place where I am comfortable sharing my home with anyone. I've let people into my heart again in the greatest of ways so I can experience love, friendship, healthy relationships, balance, vulnerability, work that's fun, and time with my family. If something comes along that doesn't align with what I want for my life, I say no. I'm worth that. All of us are.

As a result of our newfound confidence and zest for going after what we wanted and a new home that provided the perfect setting, Clare and I began hosting a gathering at our house. We needed a spiritual community, and we wanted Merit to have that experience.

We welcome all walks of life and all ways of thinking. We start with a prayer or meditation or music, then a reading or poem, then we have a discussion that stems from the reading or poem, and lastly, we set our intentions for the upcoming month. Kids are welcome to join the service or play.

We meet outdoors on the first Sunday of every month to provide spiritual and emotional support to one another, to challenge one another through our discussions, and to uplift each other. Our discussions are centered around gratitude, family dynamics, white privilege, the challenges people of color face every day, LGBTQ challenges, COVID-19 and how we've changed as a result, how to stay spiritually connected during difficult times, our different experiences of God and faith, and whatever else comes up.

Having this group in our lives has led us to many spiritual conversations with Merit and a more direct focus in teaching her what we have learned over the years.

One evening, when Merit was sitting on the toilet, she asked Clare where her dad, "Tata," was. Clare told her he was in the spirit world. Merit asked why, so Clare responded, "Because he died, and when we die our bodies go back to the earth and our spirits go to the spirit world, but we can still see and hear them, just in a different way."

The next night, I was rocking and talking with Merit, our nightly ritual. She asked me, "Is your body dying?" Feeling taken aback by the depth of her question, the words popped out of my mouth, "I am here right now."

I told her that most people die when they're older. She was worried about Clare's mom, "Nini," because Nini is old. Then she was worried about our pets, so she asked, "Is Xena dying?" Since Xena, our chihuahua, was still young and with her mother, Merit hadn't met her yet. Merit reconciled not seeing something or someone, dead or alive, by saying, "Xena is in my heart." She connected not being able to see someone with death. "God is in my heart. God is in your heart. God is in everybody's heart," she sang. I told her that we are all in each other's hearts whether we are dead or alive. She was satisfied.

The next day, Clare was outside with Merit barefoot on the ground, and Clare said to her, "Doesn't the grass feel nice on our feet, Merit?"

After a couple of seconds, she said, "Thank you, Mama God, for the grass." But when you ask Merit if God is a he or a she or a they, she always says "they" every time.

Merit has helped me remember who I am spiritually. She has brought me full circle, back to myself.

The God I was taught to revere was one that didn't sit well within my spirit as a child. I wasn't given a reference for other ways of experiencing God except through fear, shame, and unworthiness. I knew there was more, but I couldn't find my way to it. There was a deep inner calling to pull myself forward. I knew there was a way to listen to my own heart and that it would guide me to where I wanted to go.

It took pain. It took questioning everything. I knew I was held and free, but I had to take down all the walls keeping me from experiencing wholeness.

We all want to get to a place in our lives where we feel grateful and unrestricted to be who we are. We all want to feel like we can exhale.

I believe if we own who we are and are willing to share with others, our stories will connect us back to what matters.

What matters is our inner freedom. Without that, what stories are we actually sharing?

I am not saying you won't have hard days. I have hard days all the time. I am not saying you won't have fears. I still have fears around how I will be treated because I am gay. What I am saying is that you can have hard days, and you can have fears, and you can still feel limitless.

I am held and free, and so are you. Let it in.

EPILOGUE

"Our Story"

From the history of our ancestors
to the presence of our awareness,
we see a new dawn arising.

It's within you.
It's within us.

We can wait, or we can know.
We can hope, or we can believe . . .
again, in our rebirth.

Our story is one we must tell,
but not without each of us,
and not without each part.
Every moment counts—
every soul, every breath.

We know what's important,
and yet we cling
to the past and its pain
as if its perceived comfort
will free us from change.

But we are all, in here—in this—
this is our story.

Our story.

We have to tell it from the part of us
that we believe deeply in
but don't always know how to reach
or see
or touch.
It's there
beyond the details
of our shared history.

I must reach.

I must rise.

I must be willing to shed
the light within me
and leave my past behind
—to become.
To become myself for me,
for you,
for my daughter.

For my heart.
A healed heart is an open heart.

No, we aren't perfect.
Yes, we are broken . . .
in our brokenness,
our light shines through.

Grab my hand and let's walk this path to freedom.

It's where we belong.
It's where we forgive.
It's where we let go.
It's where we stand again.
And again.

ACKNOWLEDGMENTS

In creating this book, I never imagined that so many people would support me during my pre-sale campaign. You've made me believe in myself in a new way. You've made me believe in the best of us. Thank you, from the bottom of my heart.

Lanetra Brown
Deb Word
Emily Sanford
Austin Vollor
Alen Voskanian
Katie Bushby
Theresa Yong
Fonda Dichiara
Meg Baier
Paisley Hamilton
Colleen Fahey
Wendy Gibson
Tracy Maxwell
Janice Hudson
Sonny Ramaswamy
Desley Parker
Sandy Sansing
Randie Wirt

Judy McLain
Karen Richards
Joe MacGown
Jacqueline Posley
Glenda Smith
Chantz Smith
Regina Jaynes
Helen Powers
Christine Hay
Bonnie Thames
Erin Gautreau
Elisa Fuller
Linda Drake
Michael Davidson
Kim Doolittle
Kelsey Scarbrough
Damon McLeese
Pam Jones

Alexandra Hendon	Yvonne Thaxton
Pamela Blasetti	Bert Montgomery
Paul Wolfe	Robert Buckley
Ryan Brown	Amy Buckley
Shellie L Aultman	Brother Burns
Alice Eblen	D'Anne Rudden
Barbara Coats	Lindsay Kolasa
Tiffany Bailey	Blair Snively
Mariah Gibson	Maureen Whann
Lidiane M. Mocko	Carolyn Abadie
Jenna Ward	Mary A. Smith
Janae Turner	Robin Husbands
Lynn Barron	Meredith Harris
Leesa Golden	Albert Ward
Christine Arians	Dale Conner
Jonathon Breckenridge	Louise E. Davis
Kelly McNelis	Jennifer Mahne
Heather Carson	Heather Siebenaler
Jolie Niland	Regina Hyatt
Susie Utz	Kristen Haydu
Kim Caddis	Whitney Junkin
Deb Wells	Josh Whitlock
June Barnett	csunangel77
Christine Little	Hays Burchfield
Maryna Lyon	Heidi Riedesel
Will Reedy	Beth Coleman
RC Franklin	Betsy Alexander
Amy Sorrell	Dana Bailey
Kathy Dooley	William Sansing
Natalie Blanton	Allie Grant
Callye Williams	Sandra Long
Sarah Siefert	Karla Morgan

Daphne Williamson
Sarah Laughlin
Sandra Hutchins
Laura Jayne Hare
Joseph Strechay
Anna Pantano
Margaret Romney
Rachael Potts
Debbie Weaver
Donna E. Schmitz
Tunisa Rice
Tawnya Dukes
James Mozingo
Phoebe Breland
Emily Johnson
MaryRuth Caradine
Renee Ainsworth
Rosanne Radke
Lance Fremin
Natalie Langston
Lee Ann Glusenkamp
Allison Stacey Parvin
Shawn Maestretti
Mondi Mallory
Jenny Illig
Debbie Keenan
Ken Stone
Reggie Harris

Sallie Greenberg
Shanna Marroquin
Janean Romines
Robin O'Nan
Patty Lathan
Robin O'Nan
Alicia Williamson
Erin Weed
Rick Welch
Patricia Priestley
Mary Barrentine
Paula and Mike Collins
Angela Carnathan
Christy Thiel
Hope Rutagengwa
Kristi Freeman
Melanie Morel
Alison Buehler
Sarah Siler Cosby
Viveka von Rosen
Stephanie Siler
Robyn Hadden
Jess Ramsey
Arlene Olsen
Brenda McCafferty
Alicia Thompson
Eric Koester

A special thanks to Jasmine Cochran for her editing guidance, storytelling mastery, support, and friendship. She helped make this book what it is.

APPENDIX

Author's Note

Cigna and Ipsos. 2018. "Cigna U.S. Loneliness Index."
https://www.multivu.com/players/English/8294451-cigna-us-loneliness-survey/docs/IndexReport_1524069371598-173525450.pdf.

Weissbourd, Richard, Milena Batanova, Virginia Lovison, and Eric Torres. 2021. "Loneliness in America: How the Pandemic Has Deepened an Epidemic of Loneliness and What We Can Do About It." *Harvard Graduate School of Education: Making Caring Common Project*. February 2021.
https://mcc.gse.harvard.edu/reports/loneliness-in-america.

Chapter 15

O'Nan, Meagan. 2014. *Courage: Agreeing to Disagree Isn't Enough.* Columbus, Mississippi: North MS Acupuncture and Holistic Center.

APÉNDICE